DIRECT HITS

Advanced Vocabulary

Sixth Edition

For more information, please contact us by mail:

Direct Hits Publishing
2 The Prado, Unit 2, Atlanta GA 30309

Ted@DirectHitsPublishing.com

Or visit our website:
www.DirectHitsPublishing.com

Sixth Edition: August 2016

Despite our best efforts at editing and proofreading, the book may contain errors. Please feel free to contact us if you find an error, and any corrections can be found on our website.

ISBN: 978-1-936551-24-8

Written by Paget Hines
Edited by Ted Griffith
Cover Design by Carlo da Silva
Interior Design by Alison Rayner

Other Books by Direct Hits

Direct Hits Advanced Vocabulary is part of a larger series aimed at helping students improve their vocabulary. The series is designed as a progression to help students learn vocabulary as they get older, starting with *Direct Hits Essential Vocabulary*, then *Direct Hits Core Vocabulary*, and finally *Direct Hits Advanced Vocabulary*. Our books are available from Amazon, Barnes & Noble, and other major retailers.

For information on bulk orders, please email us at:
Ted@DirectHitsPublishing.com

ACKNOWLEDGEMENTS

This 6th edition reflects the collaborative efforts of an outstanding team of students, educators, reviewers, and project managers, each committed to helping young people attain their highest aspirations. Their insights and talents have been incorporated into *Direct Hits Advanced Vocabulary*.

I wish to express my gratitude to our Student Advisory Board: Tanner Hines, Kali Holliday, and Adam Liang. Their thoughtful input helped refine and update the book, keeping it readable and entertaining. Tanner was particularly helpful getting me through the last chapter of this book. His creative ideas made all the difference in the final version of the book!

Judy Martinez was vital in the editing process. She combed each page to ensure that the grammar was consistent, and she helped me simplify and condense the examples when needed.

Alison Rayner was responsible for creating our interior design. I thank her not only for her creative talent, but also for her flexibility through multiple revisions.

Additionally, I am grateful to Carlo da Silva, who once again used his artistic and graphic skills to design our distinctive cover.

Direct Hits Advanced Vocabulary would not be possible without Claire Griffith. Her vision for Direct Hits guided every aspect of this book.

A big thank you goes out to Luther Griffith for his oversight and support. I appreciate his strong and practical guidance and organization.

A special thank you to Ted Griffith, who didn't stress too much when a rogue tornado had me without power and internet on and off for a week. As always, I thank my family for their continued support, and I hope that my dad, Richard Hines, will not be too frustrated with my inclusion of the word *enfranchise*!

Paget Hines, Author

TABLE OF CONTENTS

INTRODUCTION

Why is vocabulary important, you ask?

Words are our tools for learning and communicating. A rich and varied vocabulary enables us to…

Speak more eloquently…

Describe more vividly…

Argue more compellingly…

Articulate more precisely…

Write more convincingly.

Research has proven that a powerful and vibrant vocabulary has a high correlation with success in school, business, the professions, and standardized tests including the PSAT, SAT, ACT, SSAT, and AP Exams. Yet many students complain that taking the ACT or SAT is like trying to understand a foreign language. They dread memorizing long lists of seemingly random words.

Their frustration is understandable.

Direct Hits Advanced Vocabulary offers a different approach. Each word is illustrated through relevant examples from popular movies, television, literature, music, historical events, and current headlines.

Students can place the words in a context they can easily understand and remember.

Building on the success of previous editions, the authors of *Direct Hits Advanced Vocabulary* have consulted secondary school teachers, tutors, parents, and students from around the world to ensure that these words and illustrations are exactly on target to prepare you for success on the SAT. You will find that the approach is accessible, effective, and even fun!

Direct Hits offers **selective** vocabulary using **relevant** examples with **vivid** presentation so you can achieve successful **results** on standardized tests and in life.

Let's get started!

HOW TO USE THIS BOOK

❶ The vocabulary word is always in bold print and capitalized.

❷ This is the word number, not the page number. All of the Direct Hits words are numbered in the order they appear in the Essential, Core, and Advanced books.

❸ When another Direct Hits vocabulary word is used, the word will be in bold print and capitalized. The word number (or book it is from) is inside the parentheses.

❹ The part of speech is capitalized and comes before the definition.

❺ The Pro Tip box is additional information to help expand your vocabulary knowledge.

❻ The example is written to show the vocabulary word in context.

❼ Prefix, Suffix, and/or Root box is a visual reference of word parts. The meaning is next to the word part(s) featured, and each box contains example words with definitions.

---

❷ 69 | **❶** **PRECEDENT**

❹ *NOUN—An act or instance that is used as an example in dealing with subsequent similar instances; ; a historical **PARADIGM** (Word 36)* **❸**

❺
PRO TIP
Break words into parts: *prefix, root, and/or suffix*
Pre + ced(e) + ent = precedent
Before + *go* + *n. ending* = *prior act*

Suppose you were part of a group scheduled to visit the White House and meet the President. How would you address the President, and upon meeting him (or her), what would you do? These issues have been settled by long-established **PRECEDENTS**. Washington rejected "His Highness" and "His High Mightiness" for the simple greeting "Mr. President." After saying "Mr. President, it is an honor to meet you," would you bow or shake hands? Although Washington favored bowing, Thomas Jefferson thought the practice too royal. He established the **PRECEDENT** of shaking hands, feeling that this gesture was more democratic.

❻

❼

KNOW YOUR ROOTS		
LATIN ROOT:	**CEDE**	to admit a point in an argument
CEDE	**ACCEDE**	to go along with, to agree to
CEED to go	**CONCEDE**	to yield to, agree to a loss in an election
CESS	**INTERCEDE**	to go between two litigants
	PRECEDE	to go before
	RECEDE	to go back
	SECEDE	to go apart, to leave a group, like the Union
	EXCEED	to go beyond the ordinary
	PROCEED	to go forth
	SUCCEED	to gain something good, like a goal
	ACCESSION	a going to, like an accession to the throne
	RECESSION	a going back, a decline in the economy

CHAPTER 1

Every Word Has A History

In 1922 British archaeologist Howard Carter amazed the world by discovering Pharaoh Tutankhamen's tomb. Each of the dazzling artifacts that he unearthed yielded new insights into Egyptian history.

Although we usually don't think of them in this way, words are like historic artifacts. Like the precious jewels Carter found, words also have fascinating histories. **ETYMOLOGY** (see Pro Tip on p. 21) is a branch of linguistics that specializes in digging up the origins of words.

Each word in our language has a unique history. The English language contains an especially rich collection of words derived from legends, places, customs, and names.

1 | DRACONIAN
ADJECTIVE—Characterized by very strict laws, rules, and punishments

Draco was an ancient Athenian ruler who believed that the city-state's haphazard judicial system needed to be reformed. In 621 BC, he issued a comprehensive but very severe new code of laws. Whether trivial or serious, most criminal offenses called for the death penalty. Draco's laws were so severe that they were said to be written not in ink but in blood.

Today, the word **DRACONIAN** refers to very strict laws, rules, and punishments. For example, in Iran both men and women can be stoned to death as punishment for being convicted of adultery.

2 | LACONIC, SUCCINCT, TERSE
ADJECTIVE—Very brief; concise

The ancient city-state of Sparta was located in a region of Greece called Laconia. The Spartans were fearless warriors who had little time for long speeches. As a result, they were renowned for being **LACONIC** or very concise. For example, Philip of Macedon, father of Alexander the Great, sent the Spartans a long list of demands. The **LACONIC** Spartans sent it back with a one-word answer: "No!"

Today, the word **LACONIC** still means very brief and **TERSE**.

New Englanders are often described as **LACONIC**. For instance, Robert Frost, the poet who spent most of his life in Vermont and New Hampshire, is considered the **QUINTESSENTIAL** (Word 94) **LACONIC** writer, one who expressed much in few words.

3 | SPARTAN
ADJECTIVE—Plain; simple; AUSTERE (DH Core)

The Spartans were more than just **LACONIC** (Word 2). They also prided themselves on being tough warriors who avoided luxuries and led hardy lives. For example, Spartan soldiers lived in army barracks and ate meager servings of a coarse black porridge.

Today, the word **SPARTAN** still describes a plain life without luxuries. Like the ancient Spartans, American soldiers undergo a rigorous period of training. For example, recruits at the Marine training center at Parris Island must live in **SPARTAN** barracks and endure an arduous 12-week training schedule before they can be called United States Marines.

4 | HALCYON

ADJECTIVE—Idyllically calm and peaceful; an untroubled golden time of satisfaction, happiness, and tranquility

In Greek mythology, Alcyone was the daughter of Aeolus, god of the winds, and the devoted wife of Ceyx. When Ceyx tragically drowned in a shipwreck, the distraught Alcyone threw herself into the sea. Out of compassion, the gods transformed Alcyone and Ceyx into a pair of kingfishers. The ancient Greeks named this distinctive bird *halkyon* after Alcyone. According to legend, kingfishers built a floating nest on the sea at about the time of the winter solstice in December. To protect their nest, the gods ordered the winds to remain calm for a week before and after the winter solstice. The expression "halcyon days" refers to this period of untroubled peace and tranquility.

Today, **HALCYON** still refers to a golden time of untroubled happiness and tranquility. In the movie, *The Notebook*, Allie and Noah are two carefree teenagers who meet at a local carnival on Seabrook Island, South Carolina, and spend a romantic summer together. These **HALCYON** days inspire their lifelong love for each other.

Companies can also enjoy **HALCYON** days with content employees, satisfied customers, and robust profits.

5 | SOPHISTRY

NOUN—A plausible but deliberately misleading or false argument designed to deceive someone

The Sophists were originally a respected group of ancient Greek philosophers who specialized in teaching rhetoric. However, over time they gained a reputation for their ability to persuade by using clever and often tricky arguments. Today, **SOPHISTRY** is a negative word that refers to a **PLAUSIBLE** (DH Essential) but deliberately misleading argument.

In the classic movie *Animal House*, the Deltas are a notorious group of fun-loving misfits who gleefully break campus rules. Outraged by their low grades and wild parties, Dean Wormer holds a hearing to revoke the Deltas' charter. **UNDAUNTED** (DH Core) by Dean Wormer's accusations, Otter resorts to **SOPHISTRY** in a clever but ultimately **FUTILE** (DH Core) attempt to save the Deltas:

"*Ladies and gentlemen, I'll be brief. The issue here is not whether we broke a few rules or took a few liberties with our female party guests—we did. But you can't hold a whole fraternity responsible for the behavior of a few sick, twisted individuals. For if you do, then shouldn't we blame the whole fraternity system? And if the whole fraternity system is guilty, then isn't this an indictment of our educational institutions in general? I put it to you— isn't this an indictment of our entire American society? Well, you can do whatever you want to us, but we're not going to sit here and listen to you badmouth the United States of America. Gentlemen!*"

Pleased with his **SOPHISTRY**, Otter then leads the defiant Deltas out of the chamber as all the fraternity brothers hum the "Star-Spangled Banner."

6 | CHIMERICAL

ADJECTIVE—Given to fantastic schemes; existing only in the imagination; impossible; vainly conceived

PRO TIP

CHIMERICAL is a difficult word that often appears in challenging sentence completion questions. Typically, test writers associate CHIMERICAL with once-promising medical advances that were never fully realized and were thus CHIMERICAL.

The *Chimera* was one of the most fearsome monsters in Greek mythology. A fire-breathing female, she had the head and body of a lion, a serpent's tail, and a goat's head protruding from her midsection. This frightening combination was unusually fantastic even for the ancient Greeks.

Today, a **CHIMERICAL** scheme or claim is one that is a product of un-restrained fantasy. For example, according to popular legend, Ponce de Leon discovered Florida while searching for the fabled Fountain of Youth. While the Fountain of Youth proved to be fanciful, we have still not given up our search for longevity. Fad diets, vitamin supplements, and exercise routines all offer claims that have often proved to be **CHIMERICAL.**

7 | OSTRACIZE
VERB—To deliberately exclude from a group; to BANISH

In ancient Athens, an *ostrakon* was a tile or shell. The Athenians used these shells as ballots in an annual vote to decide who, if anyone, should be banished from their city. Each voter wrote a name on his *ostrakon*. If at least 6,000 votes were cast and if a majority of them named one man, then that man was banished or **OSTRACIZED** and had to leave Athens for 10 years because he was thought to be dangerous by the state.

Today, the word **OSTRACIZE** still retains its original meaning of deliberately excluding someone from a group. For example, following World War II, angry French citizens **OSTRACIZED** people who had collaborated with the Nazis. In Chartres, vigilantes shaved the head of a young woman whose baby was fathered by a German soldier. Crowds of jeering people taunted the **OSTRACIZED** woman as she walked alone on the city streets.

8 | IMPECUNIOUS
ADJECTIVE—Poor; penniless; NOT AFFLUENT (Word 42)

When the Romans first settled the lands along the Tiber River, they lacked a metal currency. Nonetheless, Roman farmers did have an ample supply of cattle. As a result, cattle were often used as a measure of wealth. In Latin, *pecus* is the word for cattle. A Roman without a cow or *pecus* was thus **IMPECUNIOUS** or NOT WEALTHY.

Today, the word **IMPECUNIOUS** means lacking money and, thus, poor. The recent global financial crisis is considered by many to be the worst since the Great Depression. The United States' weak economy has rendered many citizens **IMPECUNIOUS**. The official unemployment rate in the United States reached a staggering 9.1 percent, a figure that did not even include the underemployed or those who had given up looking for work. Moreover, foreclosure rates were at an all-time high, leaving many Americans in a **PRECARIOUS** (DH Core) state financially.

9 | NEFARIOUS
ADJECTIVE—Famous for being wicked; ***VILLAINOUS*** *(DH Essential); vile*

In ancient Rome, the Latin word *nefarius* referred to a criminal. This unsavory connotation continued over the centuries. Today, the word **NEFARIOUS** is used to describe someone who is extremely wicked. Some of the most **NEFARIOUS** villains in film include Lord Voldemort (*Harry Potter*), the Joker (*The Dark Knight*), Darth Vader (*Star Wars*), and the Wicked Witch of the West (*The Wizard of Oz*).

10 | JOVIAL, JOCULAR
ADJECTIVE—Good-humored; cheerful

Jupiter was the chief deity of the Roman Gods. The Romans believed that each of their gods possessed particular attributes of character. As the most powerful god, Jupiter was majestic and authoritative. However, he was also believed to be fun-loving and the source of joy and happiness. Since Jupiter was also known as Jove, the word **JOVIAL** came to refer to people who have a cheerful, jolly temperament.

Today, **JOVIAL** still retains its meaning of good-humored, cheerful, and **JOCULAR**. While most people do not associate **JOVIAL** with Jupiter, they do associate the word with Santa Claus. Often referred to as "**JOVIAL** old St. Nicholas," Santa Claus is usually presented as a jolly, good-humored man who brings presents to well-behaved children.

11 | DIRGE

*NOUN—A funeral hymn; a slow, mournful, **LUGUBRIOUS** (Word 196) musical composition*

When medieval Christians gathered to pay their final respects to the deceased, the Church ceremony began with this solemn Latin phrase:

"Dirige, Domine, Deus meus, in conspectus tuo viam meam."
("Direct, O Lord my God, my way in thy sight.")

Today, a **DIRGE** refers to a sad, mournful song or hymn of lament. For example, as the Titanic slowly sank, its musicians supposedly played the **DIRGE** "Nearer, My God, To Thee" to comfort the desperate souls still on the doomed ship. As **POIGNANTLY** (DH Core) depicted in the movie, the band played the **LUGUBRIOUS DIRGE** until the very end. They then calmly went down with their ship.

12 | MAUDLIN

ADJECTIVE—Tearful; excessively sentimental

Mary Magdalene played an important and recurring role in the Gospel accounts of Christ's life and death. According to the Gospels, she stood at the foot of the cross, saw Christ laid in the tomb, and was the first recorded witness of the Resurrection. During the 15th century, artists frequently portrayed Mary Magdalene weeping as Christ was being taken down from the cross. The word **MAUDLIN** is an alteration of the name Magdalene. Today **MAUDLIN** refers to excessively sentimental behavior.

13 | QUIXOTIC

ADJECTIVE—Foolishly impractical in the pursuit of ideals; impractical idealism

Miguel de Cervantes's epic novel *Don Quixote* describes the chivalric adventures of the would-be knight Don Quixote. Motivated by chivalric ideals, Don Quixote is determined to undo the wrongs of the world.

His fertile imagination turns lonely inns into castles and windmills into fearsome giants. After a long series of misadventures, Don Quixote returns home a tired and disillusioned old man. Derived from his name, the modern word **QUIXOTIC** refers to the foolish and impractical pursuit of noble but unattainable ideals.

14 | PANDEMONIUM
NOUN—A wild uproar; tumult

PRO TIP

The prefix *PAN* is in a number of words that are ALL around you. For example, a **PANORAMIC** view enables you to see in ALL directions. A **PANACEA** is a remedy that will supposedly cure ALL diseases. A **PANOPLY** is a complete suit of armor and, thus, any covering that has ALL the necessary array of materials.

In Book I of Milton's *Paradise Lost*, the fallen Satan commands his heralds to announce: "A solemn Councel forthwith to be held/At Pandemonium, the high Capital/of Satan and his Peers." Milton **COINED** (Word 81) this name for the capital of Hell by combining the prefix *PAN*, meaning "all," with the Late Latin word *daemonium*, meaning "place of the evil spirits." As Satan's capital, Pandemonium was characterized by a place of noise, confusion, and wild uproar.

Today, the word **PANDEMONIUM** refers to a wild uproar rather than a specific place. On September 11, 2001, the terrorist attacks on the World Trade Center and the Pentagon created states of **PANDEMONIUM** in New York City and Washington, DC. Recent natural disasters have also caused significant **PANDEMONIUM**. The devastating earthquake in Haiti in January 2010 and the destructive tsunami in Japan in March 2011 caused massive uproar and panic in those countries.

15 | MARTINET
NOUN—A strict disciplinarian; a person who demands absolute adherence to forms and rules

The French King Louis XIV dreamed of winning glory by expanding France's boundaries to the Rhine River and the Alps. To achieve this goal,

Louis and his war minister, the Marquis de Louvois, created Europe's first professional army. In order to be effective, the new army required strict discipline. Louvois assigned this exacting task to Colonel Jean Martinet. A stern drillmaster, Martinet trained his troops to march in linear formations at exactly 80 paces a minute. The rigid control imposed by Martinet helped transform **NOVICE** (DH Essential) soldiers into highly-disciplined fighting units.

Today, the word **MARTINET** still refers to a strict disciplinarian. The Marine Drill Sergeants at Parris Island are renowned for being merciless **MARTINETS**. As readers of Harry Potter are well aware, **MARTINETS** are not limited to the military. In *Harry Potter and the Order of the Phoenix*, Dolores Umbridge was a **MARTINET** who tried to impose rigid standards of discipline on the students and faculty at Hogwarts.

16 | FIASCO
NOUN—A complete failure; a DEBACLE

Venetian glassblowers were renowned for their skill in making intricate glass vases and bowls. Italian etymologists explain that when a master craftsman discovered a flaw in a piece he was working on, he would turn it into an ordinary bottle to avoid wasting the glass. Since *"far fiasco"* is an Italian phrase meaning "to make a bottle," the bottle would represent a failure and, thus, a **FIASCO**.

Today, the word **FIASCO** still refers to a complete failure or **DEBACLE**. Most observers believe that the government's and BP's belated response to the 2010 Gulf Oil Spill transformed a disaster into a devastating human-made **DEBACLE**.

17 | BOWDLERIZE
VERB—To remove or delete parts of a book, song, or other work that are considered offensive; to EXPURGATE (DH Core)

Dr. Thomas Bowdler, an English physician, thought parents should read Shakespeare's plays to their children. Although Shakespeare may be an immortal bard, his plays do contain profanity and suggestive scenes that may not be appropriate for family reading. So in 1818, Bowdler decided to publish a family edition of Shakespeare. In his preface, Bowdler noted that he carefully edited "those words and expressions which cannot, with propriety, be read aloud to a family." Outraged critics attacked Bowdler and **COINED** (Word 81) the new word **BOWDLERIZE** to describe the deletion of parts of a book or play that are deemed offensive. Interestingly, the **BOWDLERIZED** edition of Shakespeare proved to be a commercial success, thus, perhaps vindicating Bowdler's judgment.

The controversy over **BOWDLERIZED** books did not end with Thomas Bowdler. In her book *The Language Police*, Diane Ravitch argues that American students are compelled to read bland texts that have been **BOWDLERIZED** by publishers and textbook committees who cut or change controversial material from books, even classics. For example, an anthology used in Tennessee schools changed "By God!" to "By gum!"

18 | GALVANIZE
VERB—To electrify; to stir into action as if with an electric shock

Luigi Galvani (1737–1790) was an Italian professor of physiology whose pioneering work stimulated important research into the nature of electricity. Galvani's name is still associated with an electrical process that puts a zinc coating over iron or steel.

One of the first uses of the word in a **METAPHORICAL** (DH Core) sense is in Charlotte Bronte's 1853 novel *Villette*: "Her approach always **GALVANIZED** him to new and spasmodic life." In more recent times Rosa Parks's simple but powerful act of protest **GALVANIZED** the people of Montgomery, Alabama, to boycott the buses, thus giving additional **IMPETUS** (DH Core) to the Civil Rights Movement.

19 | PICAYUNE
NOUN—Small value or importance; petty; trifling

The *New Orleans Times-Picayune* has one of the best-known and oddest names of an American newspaper. The word "picayune" originally referred to a small Spanish coin worth about six cents. Back in 1837, the original proprietors of the then *New Orleans Picayune* gave their new paper that name because a copy cost about six cents, or one picayune.

Today, the word **PICAYUNE** refers to something of small value and, thus, of little importance. After Hurricane Katrina, New Orleans' leaders angrily accused FEMA officials of ignoring urgent problems while they focused on minor details that could best be described as **PICAYUNE**.

20 | GERRYMANDER

NOUN—To divide a geographic area into voting districts so as to give unfair advantage to one party in elections

If you think the word **GERRYMANDER** sounds like the name of a strange political beast, you are right. The name was **COINED** (Word 81) by combining the word salamander, "a small lizard-like amphibian," with the last name of Elbridge Gerry, a former governor of Massachusetts. Gerry was immortalized in this word because an election district created by members of his party in 1812 looked like a salamander. When the famous artist Gilbert Stuart noticed the oddly-shaped district on a map in a newspaper editor's office, he decorated the outline of the district with a head, wings, and claws and then said to the editor, "That will do for a salamander!" "Gerrymander!" came the reply, and a new word was **COINED** (Word 81).

Today, the word **GERRYMANDER** still retains its meaning of an oddly-shaped district designed to favor one party. For example, California has drawn district lines so that two pockets of Republican strength in Los Angeles separated by many miles were connected by a thin strip of coastline. In this way, most Republican voters were assigned to one **GERRYMANDERED** district. District 23 is one of the narrowest districts in the United States and is often referred to as "the district that disappears at high tide."

21 | MAVERICK

NOUN—An independent individual who does not go along with a group or party; a nonconformist

Samuel A. Maverick was one of the early leaders of Texas. He fought for Texas independence, served as mayor of San Antonio, and eventually purchased a 385,000-acre ranch. While Maverick's achievements have been forgotten, his name is remembered because of his practice of refusing to brand the cattle on his ranch. These unbranded cattle were soon called *mavericks*.

Today, the meaning of the word **MAVERICK** has been extended from cattle to people. A **MAVERICK** is anyone who doesn't follow the common herd, thus, a nonconformist. In the movie *Top Gun*, Lt. Peter Mitchell received the nickname "Mav" because he was a nonconformist who did not always follow the rules.

22 | JUGGERNAUT

NOUN—An irresistible force that crushes everything in its path

Jagannath, "Lord of the World", is an incarnation of the Hindu god Vishnu. In the early 14th century, a Franciscan missionary named Friar Odoric visited India. When he returned to Europe, Odoric published a journal describing how Jagannath's devoted followers placed the god's image on an enormous carriage which they pulled through the streets. According to Odoric's inaccurate but sensational report, excited worshippers threw themselves under the carriage and were crushed to death. As Odoric's exaggerated story spread across Europe, Jagannath's name was transformed into the new word **JUGGERNAUT**.

Today, the word **JUGGERNAUT** refers to an irresistible force that crushes everything in its path. The D-Day assault forces were a **JUGGERNAUT** that crushed the German defenses.

23 | SERENDIPITY
NOUN–Discovery by fortunate accident

Sri Lanka is an island off the southeast coast of India. Known to Arab geographers as Serendip, the exotic island was the setting of a fanciful Persian fairy tale, *The Three Princes of Serendip*. The story and its title inspired the English writer Horace Walpole (1717–1797) to **COIN** (Word 81) the word **SERENDIPITY**. In a letter written in 1754, Walpole explained that **SERENDIPITY** refers to the uncanny ability of the three princes to make chance discoveries.

Today, the word **SERENDIPITY** refers to an accidental but fortunate discovery. When Scottish physician Alexander Fleming went on vacation in 1928, he left a dish smeared with Staphylococcus bacteria on a bench in his laboratory. In his absence, a mold from another lab drifted onto the culture. When Fleming returned, he noticed that the bacteria had not grown where the mold had fallen. Fleming named the active ingredient in the mold penicillin. His **SERENDIPITOUS** discovery proved to be a **WATERSHED** (Word 53) event in modern medicine. Penicillin is still one of the most effective antibiotics used around the world.

24 | NADIR
NOUN–The lowest point; the bottom

Arab astronomers called the point of the celestial sphere directly under the observer the *nazir*, or opposite. Thus, the phrase *nazir assant* meant "opposite of the zenith." With a slight modification, *nazir* entered the English language as **NADIR**.

Today the word **NADIR** is used to describe someone's (or something's) lowest point. 2015 may be considered the **NADIR** for professional sports because of widespread scandals. From the NFL's Deflategate controversy to FIFA's former President, Sepp Blatter, being charged with corruption, it seemed no sport, including fantasy gaming with DraftKings insider information allegations, was immune to serious misconduct. The public relations **NADIR** has left many spectators more **SKEPTICAL** (DH Essential) of professional sports than ever.

25 | PANACHE, VERVE, FLAMBOYANCE, ÉLAN (Word 101)
Great vigor and energy; dash, especially in artistic performance and composition

During the Middle Ages, proud European military commanders often placed feathers or a plume in their helmets as they rode into battle. Known as a *panache*, the feathers and plumes helped troops identify their commander but also made him an easier target for enemy arrows and bullets. Given the risk, it took real courage for a commander to wear a *panache*.

Today, the word **PANACHE** no longer refers to feathers or a plume. But **PANACHE** still retains its sense of **VERVE** or dash. **PANACHE** is now most frequently used to refer to **FLAMBOYANT** entertainers. For example, David Bowie was always considered one of the music world's most **FLAMBOYANT** performers.

CHAPTER 1 REVIEW

Complete each word box. The answer key is on page 140.

Great vigor and energy:

Word 1: _____

Word 2: _____

Word 3: _____

Halcyon:
List 3 synonyms: _____

Serendipity:
List 3 synonyms: _____

Fiasco:
List 3 synonyms: _____

Maverick:
List 3 synonyms: _____

Pandemonium:
List 3 synonyms: _____

Gerrymander:
Use the word in a sentence that helps explain what it means.

_____

_____

_____

Jovial:
Use the word in a sentence that helps explain what it means.

_____

_____

_____

Maudlin:
Use the word in a sentence that helps explain what it means.

_____

_____

_____

CHAPTER 2

Science And The Social Sciences

Many students believe that sophisticated words tested on AP exams or other standardized tests are obscure and rarely used by anyone except test writers. Nothing could be further from the truth. Newspapers, magazines, and Internet blogs frequently use scholarly vocabulary words. Front page headlines describe "**WATERSHED** (Word 53) events," financial articles discuss "**LUCRATIVE** (Word 38) deals," and editorials urge politicians to "reach a **CONSENSUS**" (Word 54) on important issues.

This chapter highlights 47 key words taken from science and the social sciences. While all have appeared on the standardized tests, they are also everyday words that you encounter in school and on the Internet. Since memorizing lists is inefficient and ineffective, we have provided vivid examples designed to help you make a permanent connection with each word.

A SCIENCE: TESTS TAKE YOU TO THE SCIENCE LAB AND BEYOND

26 | CATALYST

*NOUN—In chemistry, a **CATALYST** is a substance (such as an enzyme) that accelerates the rate of a chemical reaction at some temperature, but without itself being transformed or consumed by the reaction. In everyday usage a **CATALYST** is any agent that provokes or triggers change.*

Both Rosa Parks and Rachel Carson were **CATALYSTS** whose actions helped provoke historic changes. Rosa Parks's refusal to give up her bus seat acted as a **CATALYST** that helped spark the Montgomery Bus Boycott. Today, Rosa Parks is hailed as one of the pioneers of the modern civil rights movement. Rachel Carson's book *Silent Spring* was a **CATALYST** that triggered a national campaign to limit the indiscriminate use of DDT and other harmful pesticides. Today, Rachel Carson is hailed as one of the pioneers of the modern environmental movement.

27 | CAUSTIC

*ADJECTIVE—In chemistry, a **CAUSTIC** substance is one that burns or destroys organic tissue by chemical action. Hydrofluoric acid and silver nitrate are examples of **CAUSTIC** substances. In everyday usage, a **CAUSTIC** comment is one that hurts or burns.*

As a former judge on *American Idol*, Simon Cowell was famous for the **CAUSTIC** barbs he directed at **INEPT** (DH Core) contestants. He told one would-be singer, "If your lifeguard duties were as good as your singing, a lot of people would be drowning." Ouch! Now that's a **CAUSTIC** remark!

28 | CRYSTALLIZE

*VERB—In chemistry, **CRYSTALLIZATION** is the process by which crystals are formed. In everyday usage, to **CRYSTALLIZE** means to give a definite form to an idea or plan.*

There are two primary forms of intelligence—fluid and **CRYSTALLIZED**. Fluid intelligence involves being able to reason, think abstractly, and solve problems. Solving a puzzle is an excellent example of fluid intelligence as it is not based on your prior learning, experience, or education, but rather on your innate ability. **CRYSTALLIZED** intelligence reflects the storehouse of knowledge you have acquired from your formal education and personal experience. By taking the time to **METICULOUSLY** (DH Core) expand your **CRYSTALLIZED** intelligence of vocabulary meanings and grammar concepts, you can master the facts, information, and skills you need to earn a high score on the SAT and ACT.

29 | OSMOSIS

*NOUN—In chemistry, **OSMOSIS** refers to the diffusion of a fluid through a semi-permeable membrane until there is an equal concentration of fluid on both sides of the membrane. In everyday usage, **OSMOSIS** refers to a gradual, often unconscious process of assimilation.*

The scientific meaning of **OSMOSIS** is fairly straightforward: a process by which the molecules of a solvent pass through a membrane until there is an equal concentration of fluid on both sides.

OSMOSIS also has a more general meaning: it is the process of, often unconsciously, absorbing and integrating ideas and acquiring knowledge. When children learn to speak, they pick up words from repeated exposure to them. Over time, their understanding passes from hearing the words spoken by others to understanding and using the words for themselves. **FIGURATIVELY** (DH Essential), the knowledge has passed from the outside world, though the membrane of their brain, and into their memory. At this point the language spoken around them is equal to the language they know. They have learned it by **OSMOSIS**.

In a Garfield the Cat poster titled "I'm Learning By Osmosis," Garfield has tied books to his head, chest, arms, and feet in the **QUIXOTIC** (Word 13) hope that he can acquire the information they contain by **OSMOSIS**. Students will recognize the comic **IRONY** (DH Essential) suggested by the notion that knowledge can be transmitted by **PROXIMITY** (see PRO TIP, p. 35). They know that books must be opened and used repeatedly in order to learn!

30 | SEDENTARY

ADJECTIVE—In ecology, animals that are SEDENTARY remain or live in one area. In everyday usage, SEDENTARY means settled and therefore accustomed to sitting or doing little exercise.

Sloths are the slowest mammal in the world. The **SEDENTARY** creature sleeps 15 to 20 hours every day. It spends its life in treetops, usually asleep and hanging upside down. The sloth's **SEDENTARY** lifestyle leads to algae growing on its coat. Interestingly, the algae acts as a form of **CAMOUFLAGE** (DH Essential), helping to hide the motionless creature amongst the Central and South American tree canopy.

31 | VIRULENT

ADJECTIVE—In medical science, VIRULENT refers to a disease or toxin that is extremely infectious, malignant, or poisonous. In everyday usage, VIRULENT refers to language that is bitterly hostile, hateful, and antagonistic.

What do the blue-ringed octopus and the hook-nosed sea snake have in common? Both are **DIMINUTIVE** (DH Core) animals whose venom is extremely **VIRULENT**. Although only the size of a golf ball, the blue-ringed octopus can kill an adult human in minutes with its **VIRULENT** venom. Armed with venom four to eight times more **VIRULENT** than that of a cobra, the hook-nosed sea snake can easily kill almost any animal that encroaches on its territory.

On February 9, 1950, Senator Joseph McCarthy gave a **VIRULENT** speech to an audience in Wheeling, West Virginia, declaring, "I have in my hand a list of 205—a list of names known to the Secretary of State as being members of the Communist Party and who nevertheless are still working and shaping policy in the State Department."

32 | EMPIRICAL

ADJECTIVE—In science, EMPIRICAL means originating in or based on direct observation and experience. EMPIRICAL data can then be used to support or reject a hypothesis. In everyday language, EMPIRICAL means to be guided by practical experience, not theory.

The process of applying to colleges can be a daunting challenge. You should begin your search with a series of questions: Would you prefer to go to an urban college or one in a more **BUCOLIC** (DH Core) setting? Would you be more comfortable in a large state university or a small private college? These questions are only a first step. It is very important to be **EMPIRICAL**, to gather facts. Don't speculate about what a college is like or what test scores you will need. Be an **EMPIRICIST** and visit a number of colleges. On your visit, gather **EMPIRICAL** information by visiting dorms, observing classes, talking with students, and asking questions.

33 | ENTOMOLOGY

NOUN—The scientific study of insects

How are beekeepers and CSI investigators connected? Both use **ENTOMOLOGY** to solve problems.

Several winters have witnessed the sudden disappearance of more than 33 percent of the western honeybee population. **ENTOMOLOGISTS** are

> **PRO TIP**
>
> Many students confuse **ENTOMOLOGY** with **ETYMOLOGY**. **ENTOMOLOGY** is the study of insects, while **ETYMOLOGY** is a branch of linguistics concerned with the history and derivation of words.

mystified by what is officially called Colony Collapse Disorder (CCD). According to the Agricultural Research Service, honeybees are not **INDIGENOUS** (DH Core) to the New World; they were brought from Europe and are responsible for pollinating many agricultural crops as well as plant communities in the wild. For example, almonds are completely dependent on honeybees for pollination. Could the honeybee decline be explained by the fact that they are not **ENDEMIC** (DH Core), or are there environmental causes? The answer remains a **DISQUIETING** (Word 181) **ENIGMA** (DH Core) that **ENTOMOLOGISTS** are anxious to solve before our agriculture industry is **DELETERIOUSLY** (DH Core) affected.

Forensic **ENTOMOLOGISTS** are trained to investigate suspicious deaths by analyzing the presence of insects at crime scenes. By noting the types of insects and their colonization patterns, the **ENTOMOLOGISTS** can deduce where a body decomposed, determine whether it was moved, and even uncover gaps in the crime timeline.

34 | GESTATE

*VERB—In science, **GESTATE** means to carry within the uterus from conception to delivery. In everyday language, **GESTATE** means to conceive and develop in the mind.*

Periods of **GESTATION** vary from animal to animal. For example, the period of **GESTATION** for domesticated cats and dogs is two months. In contrast, the period of **GESTATION** for elephants is almost 22 months!

Ideas, like a fetus, often require time to **GESTATE**. For example, the ideas contained in the Declaration of Independence did not suddenly spring from Jefferson's mind onto a piece of parchment. He later acknowledged that his eloquent statements about natural rights were derived from the English philosopher John Locke and had been **GESTATING** in his mind for some time.

35 | CATHARTIC
ADJECTIVE—Purgative, either physically or emotionally; cleansing

The medical meaning of a **CATHARTIC**, as a laxative or purgative drug or agent, has widened to encompass a more psychological meaning suggesting an emotional cleansing or discharge of pent-up feelings.

Aristotle, the ancient Greek philosopher and literary critic, used the noun **CATHARSIS** to describe the relief or purging of emotions that the audience felt at the end of a Greek tragedy. The two most important emotions that were aroused during Greek plays were "pity" and "terror." Aristotle thought that *Oedipus Rex* was the **QUINTESSENTIAL** (Word 94) tragedy, for the king at the end must accept that he has inadvertently committed all the crimes that he has sought to avoid. Thus, he is a tragic hero. The audience leaves the theater saddened by the outcome but satisfied that the only appropriate resolution has occurred.

36 | PARADIGM
NOUN—In science, a PARADIGM is a framework or model of thought

In 1610, the Italian astronomer and physicist Galileo Galilei did something no other human being had ever done before. He pointed a telescope at Jupiter and observed the orbits of four of its moons. Galileo realized that the force (which we now call gravity) that kept the moons of Jupiter in their orbits was the same force keeping the Earth and the other planets in their orbits around the Sun. Galileo's scientific observations refuted the old geocentric **PARADIGM** that the Sun and all the planets revolve around the Earth. Instead, Galileo offered scientific support for Copernicus's revolutionary new heliocentric **PARADIGM** that placed the Sun in the center of the solar system. Galileo's work triggered a **MOMENTOUS** (DH Core) **PARADIGM** shift in human thought.

B   ECONOMICS: THESE WORDS ARE ABOUT DOLLARS AND SENSE

37 | ENTREPRENEUR
NOUN–A person who organizes and manages a business or enterprise

Mark Zuckerberg is an American **ENTREPRENEUR** who is the co-founder of Facebook. Zuckerberg launched Facebook from his Harvard dorm room on February 4, 2004. Facebook now has over one billion users and generates over $4 billion in revenue a year. As a result, Zuckerberg is one of the youngest billionaires in the world.

Although Zuckerberg is an **ENTREPRENEUR**, he is not an **INNOVATOR** (DH Core). Zuckerberg borrowed his original concept from a product produced by his prep school, Phillips Exeter Academy. For decades, the school published and distributed a printed manual for all its students and faculty, unofficially called the "face book." However, Zuckerberg was **PRESCIENT** (Word 184). Like other Internet pioneers, he understood the power of the Web to create an interactive community of users, and in 2010 *Vanity Fair* magazine named him #1 on its list of the Top 100 "most influential people of the Information Age."

38 | LUCRATIVE
ADJECTIVE–Very profitable

Celebrities **COVET** (DH Core) lead roles in popular TV programs not only for the fame they bring but also for their **LUCRATIVE** salaries. For example, Ashton Kutcher, who replaced Charlie Sheen on *Two and a Half Men*, earns $700,000 per episode, the largest salary of any comedy TV actor. Reality show stars also receive extremely **LUCRATIVE** salaries. Mariah Carey, Keith Urban, and Nicki Minaj each received a multi-million dollar contract to be a judge on *American Idol*.

39 | EXTRAVAGANT

ADJECTIVE—Excessive and therefore lacking restraint

The Bugatti Veyron EB 16.4 is the world's most powerful and **EXTRAVAGANT** car. The Veyron's 1200 horsepower engine can accelerate from 0 to 60 mph in just 2.4 seconds and 0 to 100 mph in 5.0 seconds. The open-top Grand Sport Vitesse is the fastest street-legal production car in the world. Of course, the Veyron also consumes an **EXTRAVAGANT** amount of fuel, getting just under 6 mpg in city driving. At full throttle, the Veyron would empty its 26-gallon fuel tank in just 12 minutes. How much does this **EXTRAVAGANT** car cost? It can be yours for $2,400,000!

40 | AVARICE, CUPIDITY

*NOUN—Excessive desire for wealth; greed; **COVETOUSNESS** (DH Core)*

Philosophers and religious leaders have long condemned **AVARICE**. The Greek philosopher Aristotle demonstrated his deep understanding of human nature when he wrote, "The **AVARICE** of mankind is insatiable." During the Middle Ages, Christian theologians identified **AVARICE** as one of the seven deadly sins.

Charles Ponzi (1882–1949) was the **EPITOME** (Word 94) of **AVARICE**. In 1903, he arrived in America by his own account "with $2.51 in his pocket and $1 million in hopes." It was his **AVARICE** that drove him in a criminal direction most of his life. In the early 1920s, he swindled many individuals by promising a 50 percent profit in 45 days or 100 percent within 90 days, by buying discounted postal reply coupons in other countries and redeeming them at face value in the United States. In reality, Ponzi was paying his early investors with money from his later investors. As his original investors touted their success with Ponzi, his pool of investors rapidly expanded, and he hired agents to act on his behalf. As his base grew and individuals reinvested their profits with him, he eventually was able to control the Hanover Trust Bank of Boston.

His **AVARICE** enabled him to live in an **OPULENT** (DH Essential) mansion with air-conditioning and heated swimming pool in the 1920s. His success brought the scrutiny of newspaper reporters and, through a variety of twists and turns, his **CUPIDITY** was discovered. Investors eventually lost $20 million. This type of scheme is now known as a "Ponzi scheme." In 2009, Bernie Madoff pleaded guilty to operating a Ponzi scheme that had losses estimated to be $65 billion, making it the largest investor fraud in history.

41 | GLUT, PLETHORA, SURFEIT
NOUN—A surplus or excess of something

While our used-car lots now have a **GLUT** of gas-guzzling vehicles, our landfills are filling up with a **PLETHORA** of old computers, printers, TVs, and other unwanted consumer electronic goods. Americans are now throwing away two million tons of electronic trash, or e-waste, each year. While there is a **SURFEIT** of outdated e-waste, there is currently a **PAUCITY** (DH Core) of recycling options. The Environmental Protection Agency estimates that we recycle only 350,000 tons of e-waste each year.

42 | DESTITUTE, IMPOVERISHED, INDIGENT
ADJECTIVE—Very poor, lacking basic resources
AFFLUENT
ADJECTIVE—Very rich, having abundant resources

In the movie *Trading Places*, Eddie Murphy's character was originally **DESTITUTE** but became very **AFFLUENT**. In the movie *Coming to America*, Murphy played an African prince who pretended to be **IMPOVERISHED** but had in fact grown up in an **OPULENT** (DH Essential) palace.

Eddie Murphy's characters were both fictional. In the movie *The Pursuit of Happyness*, Will Smith portrayed the real life story of how Chris

Gardner lost all of his family's savings by investing in a franchise selling bone density scanners. As a result, Chris became **INDIGENT**, and he and his young son were forced to spend nights riding buses and sleeping in subway restrooms. Chris ultimately became **AFFLUENT** by learning how to become a successful stock broker.

43 | MUNIFICENT
ADJECTIVE—Very generous

As the founder and CEO of Microsoft Corporation, Bill Gates has been primarily known as a technologist and **ENTREPRENEUR** (Word 37), but in 1994, Gates laid the groundwork for the next phase of his life by making a $94 million gift to the William H. Gates Foundation. The foundation was established to provide financial assistance to **PHILANTHROPIC** (DH Core) organizations that work to improve global healthcare and reduce poverty. Over the ensuing years, Gates continued his **MUNIFICENT** support to the foundation to such a degree that by the time he retired from Microsoft and assumed full-time responsibilities at the foundation, it had over $29 billion in assets. When his wife, Melinda, joined him at the foundation, it was renamed the Bill and Melinda Gates Foundation. Because of their continued **MUNIFICENCE** to global causes, Bill and Melinda Gates are considered two of the world's leading **PHILANTHROPISTS** (DH Core).

44 | PARSIMONIOUS
ADJECTIVE—Excessively cheap with money; stingy

Would you want people to call you a "Scrooge"? Probably not. Ebenezer Scrooge is the leading character in *A Christmas Carol* by Charles Dickens. Scrooge lived up to his name by being very **PARSIMONIOUS**. A **PARSIMONIOUS** person would be the **ANTITHESIS** (DH Core) of someone who is **MUNIFICENT** (Word 43).

45 | DEPRECIATION

NOUN—Any decrease or loss in value caused by age, wear, or market conditions

DEPRECIATION means that values are going down! The stock market crash of 1929 caused a severe **DEPRECIATION** in the value of stocks. By 1932, stocks listed on the New York Stock Exchange were worth just 11 percent of their pre-crash value. **DEPRECIATION** is not limited to historic examples found only in textbooks. In the last two years, American homeowners collectively lost more than $2 trillion in home value as their properties **DEPRECIATED**.

46 | REMUNERATE

VERB—To compensate; to make payment for; to pay a person

REMUNERATION varies greatly from job to job. On July 24, 2009, the federal minimum wage rose from $6.55 per hour to $7.25 per hour. The President of the United States earns $400,000 per year, and the Vice President earns $230,700. In contrast, in 2015 boxer Floyd Mayweather was the top paid athlete in the world, having earned approximately $300 million.

C HISTORY AND GEOGRAPHY: THESE WORDS WILL HELP YOU UNDERSTAND PEOPLE, PLACES, AND EVENTS

47 | ACCORD

NOUN—A formal concurrence, agreement, or harmony of minds

In *Pirates of the Caribbean: The Curse of the Black Pearl*, Captain Jack Sparrow and Will reach an **ACCORD**. Will agrees to free Sparrow, and then Sparrow agrees to help Will find Elizabeth. In world affairs, nations also sign **ACCORDS**. For example, the Helsinki **ACCORDS** (1975) recognized basic human rights, and the Camp David **ACCORDS** (1978) provided a framework for establishing peaceful relations between Egypt and Israel. The Dayton **ACCORDS** (1995) ended the war in Bosnia and established peace and stability in Bosnia and Herzegovina.

48 | ENLIGHTEN, EDIFY

VERB—To inform, instruct, illuminate, remove darkness and ignorance

ERUDITE

ADJECTIVE—Learned, literate, or authoritative

During the Enlightenment, writers such as Voltaire **ENLIGHTENED** European society by urging people to use science and reason instead of blindly following inherited prejudices. Voltaire took it upon himself to **EDIFY** France single-handedly. He wrote about 70 volumes of various kinds of literature. He was considered one of the most **ERUDITE** thinkers of his time.

In cartoons and comics, a light bulb appears over someone's head when the person suddenly understands something because he or she is **ENLIGHTENED**!

49 | APPEASEMENT

NOUN—The policy of granting concessions to maintain peace

Would you **APPEASE** a crying child by giving him or her a piece of candy? Would you **APPEASE** a bully who threatened to beat you up? Are there times when **APPEASEMENT** is a wise policy? The British Prime Minister Neville Chamberlain thought so. At the Munich Conference in September 1938, Chamberlain **APPEASED** Hitler by agreeing to his demand to control the Sudetenland. When he returned to London, Chamberlain told cheering crowds, "I believe it is peace for our time." Chamberlain's prediction proved to be tragically wrong.

50 | NULLIFY

VERB—To make null; to declare invalid

The tariffs of 1828 and 1832 infuriated John C. Calhoun of South Carolina. Led by Calhoun, South Carolina voted to **NULLIFY** or invalidate the tariffs. President Jackson rejected **NULLIFICATION** by saying that it was treason and that those implementing it were traitors. The crisis was averted when Henry Clay devised a compromise in which the tariffs were gradually lowered.

51 | TRIUMVIRATE

NOUN—A group or association of three leaders

John C. Calhoun, Henry Clay, and Daniel Webster were a group of three American statesmen known as "The Great Triumvirate," who dominated the U.S. Senate during the 1830s and 1840s. While the term **TRIUMVIRATE** usually refers to political leaders, it can be used to describe any group of three (the prefix *tri* means three). For example, the videogame console market is dominated by the **TRIUMVIRATE** of Nintendo, Sony, and Microsoft.

52 | PRETEXT

NOUN—An excuse; an alleged cause

On August 2 and 4, 1964, two American destroyers patrolling international waters in the Gulf of Tonkin reported that they had been fired upon by North Vietnamese PT boats. Although later investigations strongly suggested that the North Vietnamese fired in self-defense on August 2 and the "attack" of August 4 never happened, President Johnson used the alleged attacks as a **PRETEXT** to ask Congress for broader powers. The **PRETEXT** worked. Congress promptly passed the *Tonkin Gulf Resolution*, giving Johnson a blank check to escalate the war in Southeast Asia.

53 | WATERSHED

NOUN—Critical point that marks a change of course; a turning point

This generation of Americans has experienced a **WATERSHED** event that riveted the entire nation and marked a crucial historic turning point. On January 20, 2009, a record crowd of approximately 1.5 million people watched Chief Justice John Roberts swear in Barack Obama as the 44th President of the United States. The inauguration of America's first African-American president marked an historic **WATERSHED** in American history. For millions of people in the United States and around the world, the inauguration marked the fulfillment of Dr. King's dream and the beginning of a new era in American political history.

54 | CONSENSUS

NOUN—A general agreement

Some states, like California, place propositions on election ballots dealing with issues from tax increases to capital punishment. If passed by voter **CONSENSUS**, a proposition, or ballot initiative, can modify the articles of California's Constitution. Note that a **CONSENSUS** does not mean that everyone must be in complete agreement with a policy or a decision. Propositions can be passed in California by simple majority, not the two-thirds **CONSENSUS** needed to amend the U.S. Constitution.

55 | AUTOCRAT, DESPOT

NOUN—A ruler or other person with unlimited power and authority

In the movie *300*, Xerxes is portrayed as an **AUTOCRAT** who is determined to conquer and enslave the freedom-loving Greeks. However, led by Sparta and Athens, the Greeks successfully defeat Xerxes, thus defending democracy. The modern world still has countries ruled by **AUTOCRATS**. For example, Omar Hassan Al-Bashir has wielded absolute power over Sudan since 1989. The **AUTOCRATIC** Bashir brutally suppresses all opposition. Because of his war crimes in Darfur, he is the only world leader that has a warrant out for his arrest by the International Criminal Court.

56 | MANIFESTO

NOUN—A public declaration of beliefs, policies, or intentions

MANIFESTOS are not written by people who are self-satisfied and complacent. They are written by people who are **INDIGNANT** (DH Essential) and demand a change. For example, in 1848 a small but determined group of feminists held a Women's Rights Convention at Seneca Falls, New York. Led by the defiant Elizabeth Cady Stanton, they issued a **MANIFESTO** called the "Declaration of Sentiments," which boldly declared that "all men and women are created equal." The **MANIFESTO** launched the modern women's rights movement.

57 | ENFRANCHISE

VERB—To endow with the rights of citizenship, especially the right to vote

DISENFRANCHISE

VERB—To deprive of some privilege or right, especially the right to vote

In American history, Jim Crow laws **DISENFRANCHISED** African-American voters, while the Voting Rights Act of 1965 **ENFRANCHISED** African-American voters. Ratified in 1920, the 19th Amendment **ENFRANCHISED** millions of American women. The 26th Amendment **ENFRANCHISED** 18-year-old American citizens.

58 | COERCE

VERB—To force to act or think in a certain way by use of pressure, threats, or torture; to compel

Joseph Stalin ruled the Soviet Union as an **AUTOCRAT** (Word 55) from 1924 until his death in 1953. Stalin used terror to **COERCE** the Russian people to unquestioningly follow his leadership. In the *Gulag Archipelago*, Alexander Solzhenitsyn describes a Communist Party conference in which officials respond to a call for a tribute to Comrade Stalin with "stormy applause." The ovation continued because secret police "were standing in the hall applauding and waiting to see who would quit first!" The threat of **COERCION** worked: "The applause went on—six, seven, eight minutes!" Finally, after 11 minutes the director of a paper factory stopped applauding and sat down. Solzhenitsyn explains, "That was how they discovered who the independent people were." In a frightening demonstration of **COERCION**, the authorities arrested the factory director and sentenced him to 10 years in a labor camp. In a chilling reminder of the power of a totalitarian state to **COERCE** conformity, the interrogator reminded the former factory director, "Don't ever be the first to stop applauding."

59 | EGALITARIAN

ADJECTIVE—Favoring social equality; believing in a society in which all people have equal political, economic, and civil rights

During the 19th century, American utopian leaders were inspired by a dream of creating **EGALITARIAN** communities. Founded in 1848 by John Humphrey Noyes, the Oneida Community in upstate New York became a flourishing **EGALITARIAN** commune of some 300 people. Men and women shared equally in all the community's tasks, from field to factory to kitchen. The members lived in one building and ate in a common dining hall. The dream of **EGALITARIAN** living did not last. The communal dining hall ultimately became a restaurant. Led by Noyes's son, Pierrepont, Oneida Community, Ltd. grew into the world's leading manufacturer of stainless steel knives, forks, and spoons, with annual sales of a half-billion dollars.

60 | DEMARCATION

NOUN—The setting or marking of boundaries or limits, as a line of demarcation

What is the relationship between the word **DEMARCATION** and the reason Brazil is the only Portuguese-speaking country in the Americas? Columbus's **WATERSHED** (Word 53) voyage created an **ACRIMONIOUS** (DH Core) dispute between Spain and Portugal over the rights to lands in the New World. The two nations avoided an **IMPASSE** (DH Core) by agreeing to the 1494 Treaty of Tordesillas. Under the terms of this agreement, Spain and Portugal divided the non-Christian world into two zones of influence. The line of **DEMARCATION** gave Portugal a claim to Brazil.

61 | INQUISITION

NOUN—A severe interrogation; a systematic questioning

The **INQUISITION** was a formal court of justice established (1232-1820) by the Roman Catholic Church to discover and suppress false beliefs. Although the United States has never had a formal court of **INQUISITION**, numerous zealots have conducted **INQUISITIONS** into the conduct of public officials. The best known of these **INQUISITIONS** was conducted by Senator Joseph McCarthy during the early 1950s. McCarthy ruthlessly questioned public officials as part of his campaign against alleged Communists. Instigated by McCarthyism, Hollywood "blacklists" unfairly stigmatized screenwriters, actors, and directors as Communist sympathizers.

62 | AMELIORATE

VERB—To make a situation better

EXACERBATE

VERB—To make a situation worse

Dorothea Dix, Ida B. Wells-Barnett, and Batman were crusaders who dedicated themselves to **AMELIORATING** social problems. Dorothea Dix worked to **AMELIORATE** the lives of the **INDIGENT** (Word 42) insane by creating the first generation of American mental hospitals. Ida B. Wells-Barnett worked to **AMELIORATE** the lives of African-Americans by exposing the problem of lynching in the South. And Batman worked to **AMELIORATE** the lives of the citizens of Gotham City by fighting the power of its crime bosses. Interestingly, Batman learned that, **PARADOXICALLY** (DH Core), his efforts also **EXACERBATED** Gotham's crime problem by leading to an escalation of violence.

63 | DESICCATED
ADJECTIVE—Thoroughly dried out; lifeless, totally arid

Antarctica is technically a desert that receives less than two inches of precipitation a year. One interior region of the Antarctic is known as the Dry Valleys. These valleys have not seen rainfall in over two million years. The Dry Valleys exist because 100 mph Katabatic downwinds **DESICCATE** all moisture. The freezing temperatures and the absence of water and all life simulate conditions on the Planet Mars. As a result, the region is used as a training ground for astronauts who may one day make a voyage to the equally-**DESICCATED** Red Planet.

64 | CONTIGUOUS
ADJECTIVE—Sharing an edge or boundary; touching

PRO TIP

CONTIGUOUS means that two objects actually touch. In contrast, **PROXIMITY** means that two objects are very near in space or time. On a city street, two **CONTIGUOUS** businesses touch each other, while two businesses separated by other stores share a close **PROXIMITY** to each other.

Which of the following is the southern-most city in the 48 **CONTIGUOUS** states?

A) Kaalualu, Hawaii

B) Key West, Florida

The answer depends upon the meaning of the word **CONTIGUOUS**. Since the 48 **CONTIGUOUS** or touching states do not include Hawaii (or Alaska), the correct answer is B. Hawaii is actually an archipelago located in the central Pacific Ocean about 2,000 miles southwest of the 48 **CONTIGUOUS** states.

D LAW AND ORDER: THESE WORDS WILL HELP YOU UNDERSTAND HOW THE WHEELS OF JUSTICE TURN

65 | PERTINENT

ADJECTIVE—Relevant; to the point; clearly illustrative of a major point

Elon Musk, co-founder of PayPal and Tesla Motors, founded his third company, Space Explorations Technologies (Space-X), to focus on advancing the state of rocket technology. Recently, NASA awarded a contract to Space-X to replace the cargo transportation function to the space shuttle. As part of the contract, NASA and Space-X share **PERTINENT** information to enable the Space-X launch vehicle to safely dock with the international shuttle.

In 2006, Steve Jobs placed the **PROTOTYPE** (DH Core) of the iPhone in his pocket along with his keys. The iPhone had a hard plastic surface for the display that became scratched by his keys. Given Jobs's **METICULOUS** (DH Core) attention to details, he knew this would be a big problem. During a phone call between Jobs and the CEO of Corning Glass, Wendell Weeks, Weeks shared **PERTINENT** information about the 1960 Gorilla Glass project that solved the problem. Corning Glass had experimented with chemically strengthened glass in 1960 and developed the predecessor of what is now known as Gorilla Glass, a tough, scratch-resistant material. Aside from being used in a hundred racecars, the product had no practical application at the time. Jobs was the first to use Gorilla Glass in the iPhone with tremendous success, and it is now used in over 20 percent of smart phones and other electronic devices worldwide.

66 | COMPLICITY

NOUN—Association or participation in a wrongful act

Tupac Shakur is widely believed to be one of America's greatest and most successful rappers, with 75 million albums sold worldwide and over 50 million in the United States. On September 7, 1996, Shakur was shot four times in a drive-by shooting in Las Vegas. He died six days later. Because of their bitter rivalry with Tupac, rappers Biggie Smalls and Sean Combs were suspected of being **COMPLICIT** in the murder. However, both Biggie and Combs vigorously denied any **COMPLICITY** in Tupac's death. Despite many investigations, the case remains unsolved. Sadly, Tupac's mother passed away in May 2016, so she never found the answers she wanted about her son's death in her lifetime.

67 | EXONERATE, EXCULPATE
VERB—To free from guilt or blame

What do Benjamin Franklin Gates (*National Treasure: Book of Secrets*) and Harry Potter have in common? They both **EXONERATED** members of their families of **EXECRABLE** (Word 183) crimes. Ben successfully **EXCULPATED** his great-great-grandfather, Thomas Gates, of **COMPLICITY** (Word 66) in the plot to assassinate Abraham Lincoln. Harry successfully **EXONERATED** his godfather, Sirius Black, of the murder of Peter Pettigrew and 12 Muggles.

68 | INDISPUTABLE
ADJECTIVE—Not open to question; undeniable; irrefutable

Who killed President Kennedy? The Warren Commission published a comprehensive report providing what it believed was **INDISPUTABLE** evidence that Lee Harvey Oswald acted alone. However, **SKEPTICS** (DH Essential) soon criticized the Warren Commission's findings. In the movie *JFK*, director Oliver Stone presents what he considers **INDISPUTABLE** evidence that Lee Harvey Oswald was, in fact, part of a secret conspiracy to kill President Kennedy.

69 | PRECEDENT

NOUN—An act or instance that is used as an example in dealing with subsequent similar instances; ; a historical PARADIGM (Word 36)

PRO TIP

Break words into parts: *prefix, root, and/or suffix*

Pre	+	ced(e)	+	ent	=	precedent
Before	+	*go*	+	*n. ending*	=	*prior act*

Suppose you were part of a group scheduled to visit the White House and meet the President. How would you address the President, and upon meeting him (or her), what would you do? These issues have been settled by long-established **PRECEDENTS**. Washington rejected "His Highness" and "His High Mightiness" for the simple greeting "Mr. President." After saying "Mr. President, it is an honor to meet you," would you bow or shake hands? Although Washington favored bowing, Thomas Jefferson thought the practice too royal. He established the **PRECEDENT** of shaking hands, feeling that this gesture was more democratic.

KNOW YOUR ROOTS

LATIN ROOT:			
CEDE **CEED** **CESS**	to go	**CEDE**	to admit a point in an argument
		ACCEDE	to go along with, to agree to
		CONCEDE	to yield to, agree to a loss in an election
		INTERCEDE	to go between two litigants
		PRECEDE	to go before
		RECEDE	to go back
		SECEDE	to go apart, to leave a group, like the Union
		EXCEED	to go beyond the ordinary
		PROCEED	to go forth
		SUCCEED	to gain something good, like a goal
		ACCESSION	a going to, like an accession to the throne
		RECESSION	a going back, a decline in the economy

70 | UNPRECEDENTED

ADJECTIVE—Without previous example, never known before

Musician, television actor, and film star Will Smith has achieved **UNPRECEDENTED** success. Even as a teenager, Smith demonstrated a **PENCHANT** (DH Core) for show business as a moderately successful rapper. In 1990, he crossed over to television when he landed a lead role on the hit show *The Fresh Prince of Bel-Air*, launching his career as an actor. From 2002 to 2008, Smith released eight consecutive films that grossed over $100 million worldwide. This **UNPRECEDENTED** achievement established him as one of the most marketable stars in Hollywood.

Smith took a **HIATUS** (Word 186) from acting to foster the **BURGEONING** (Word 117) careers of his children, Jaden and Willow, but returned four years later to the top of the charts with *Men in Black 3*. With a **SPATE** (Word 172) of upcoming films in the works, Smith is poised to continue his **PROLIFIC** (Word 166) career.

71 | MALFEASANCE

NOUN—Misconduct or wrongdoing, especially by a public official; intentionally performing an act that is illegal

MALFEASANCE by political officials can range from seemingly minor acts to the outlandish. A local city council person hiring his niece for a position at a salary level in excess of the norm and encouraging the niece to record more hours than she actually worked would be an act of **MALFEASANCE**. Illinois Governor Rod Blagojevich was charged and found

> **PRO TIP**
>
> **MALFEASANCE** is a legal term that is based on two other legal concepts: **MISFEASANCE** and **NONFEASANCE**. **MISFEASANCE** is performing a perfectly legal act, but in a mistaken or erroneous manner. For example, the accountant's **MISFEASANCE** was sending out an invoice to a customer that had the wrong items on it. **NONFEASANCE** is the failure to act when the position one occupies requires one to act. For example, the police officer committed an act of **NONFEASANCE** when he failed to arrest the driver for running through a red light.

guilty of **MALFEASANCE** for trying to unmistakably sell the U.S. Senate seat vacated by then President-elect Barack Obama for a large sum of money.

72 | PROBITY
NOUN—Integrity and uprightness; honesty; high moral standards

George Washington had a reputation for **PROBITY** based on the story of his refusal to lie about chopping down the cherry tree.

Even though historians now think the story is **APOCRYPHAL** (Word 129), made up by a pastor to sell books, in 1789 George Washington was unanimously elected as the first president of the United States of America because of his **PROBITY**. He is the only president to ever receive 100 percent of the electoral votes.

The first United States Congress voted to pay Washington a salary of $25,000 a year, a large sum in 1789. Since Washington was already a wealthy man, he declined to accept the salary. Congress urged him to reconsider and accept the compensation. He **ACQUIESCED** (DH Core) in order not to set the **PRECEDENT** (Word 69) that one needed to be wealthy in order to be president. He wanted to make sure the titles and trappings of the office were suitably republican and never emulated the European royal courts. For example, he preferred the title "Mr. President" to some of the more lofty names suggested. Congressman Henry "Light-Horse Harry" Lee, a Revolutionary War comrade of Washington's, famously **EULOGIZED** (DH Core) Washington: "First in war, first in peace, and first in the hearts of his countrymen; he was second to none in the humble and enduring scenes of private life; pious, just, humane, temperate, and **SINCERE** (DH Core); uniform, dignified, and commanding, his example was edifying to all around him as were the effects of that example lasting."

CHAPTER 2 REVIEW

Complete each word box. The answer key is on page 140.

Excessive desire for wealth:

Word 1: _____

Word 2: _____

Word 3: _____

Very poor:

Word 1: _____

Word 2: _____

Word 3: _____

Catalyst:
Definition in your own words: _____

_____

Nullify:
Definition in your own words: _____

_____

Complicity:
List 3 synonyms: _____

Coerce:
List 3 synonyms: _____

Sedentary:
List 3 synonyms: _____

Affluent:
List 3 synonyms: _____

Watershed:
Use the word in a sentence that helps explain what it means.

_____

_____

Probity:
Use the word in a sentence that helps explain what it means.

_____

_____

CHAPTER 3

Words With Multiple Meanings

Learning new vocabulary words is a challenge when a word has a single meaning. Many students are surprised to discover that there are words that have multiple meanings. For example, everyone knows that a **FLAG** (Word 78) is a rectangular piece of fabric with a distinctive design that is used to symbolize a nation. But **FLAG** can also mean to lose energy or interest.

Test writers have long been aware of words with multiple meanings. Students who know only one of the meanings often eliminate the word and miss the question. In fact, words like **FLAG** and **CHECK** (Word 77) are among the most-missed words on the standardized tests like the ACT, SAT, and GRE.

This chapter will examine and illustrate 22 commonly-used words with multiple meanings. Our focus will be on these words' secondary definitions, the ones test writers use to test your knowledge. So be prepared to learn that everyday words like **CHECK**, **COIN** (Word 81), and even **PEDESTRIAN** (Word 88) have less commonly-used secondary meanings.

73 | ARREST

VERB—To bring to a stop; to halt

What is the first thing you think of when you hear the word **ARREST**? For most, **ARREST** probably calls to mind a police officer and handcuffs. **ARREST** does mean to seize and hold under the authority of the law.

The word **ARREST** has other meanings. Test writers will use **ARREST** to mean to bring to a stop or halt. Environmentalists, for example, hope to **ARREST** the growth of carbon dioxide emissions in the Earth's atmosphere. One way to remember this use of **ARREST** is to think of a cardiac **ARREST**. This condition takes place when there is an abrupt stoppage of normal blood circulation due to heart failure.

74 | GRAVITY

NOUN—Seriousness; dignity; solemnity; weight

Everyone has heard the expression, "What goes up must come down." This saying is true because of the law of **GRAVITY**. In physics, **GRAVITY** refers to the natural force of attraction exerted by a celestial body.

On October 22, 1962, President Kennedy informed a stunned nation that the Soviet Union had **SURREPTITIOUSLY** (DH Core) placed intermediate-range nuclear missiles in Cuba. The President underscored the **GRAVITY** of the crisis when he ordered a naval blockade of Cuba and sternly warned that the United States would react to any missile launched from Cuba with a "full retaliatory response upon the Soviet Union."

75 | PRECIPITATE

VERB—To cause, to bring about prematurely, hastily, or suddenly; impulsive

Most people associate the word **PRECIPITATION** with rain, snow, or sleet. However, **PRECIPITATE** can also refer to a result or outcome of an action. Test writers often use **PRECIPITATE** on AP U.S. History questions, as when the discovery of Soviet missiles in Cuba **PRECIPITATED** the Cuban Missile Crisis.

In chemistry, a **PRECIPITATE** is a substance that separates out of a solution or a result of a chemical reaction.

76 | RELIEF

NOUN—Elevation of a land surface
NOUN—A feeling of reassurance or relaxation

What is the first thing that comes to your mind when you hear the word **RELIEF**? In everyday usage, **RELIEF** most commonly refers to the feeling of ease when a burden has been removed or lightened. For example, in baseball a **RELIEF** pitcher eases the burden of the starting pitcher.

However, **RELIEF** can also be used as a geographic term that refers to the elevation of a land surface. For example, **RELIEF** maps of the United States rise at the Appalachian Mountains in the East and at the Rocky Mountains in the West.

77 | CHECK

VERB—To restrain; halt; hold back; contain

We are all familiar with the word **CHECK**. We earn **CHECKS**, cash **CHECKS**, and **CHECK** our work on math problems. Airline passengers **CHECK** in at the ticket counter, and hotel guests **CHECK** in at the registration counter. Test writers know that you are familiar with these everyday uses of the word **CHECK**.

But the word **CHECK** can also mean to restrain, halt, or hold back. For example, our Constitution calls for a system of **CHECKS** and balances to restrain each branch of government. During the Cold War, the U.S. policy of containment was designed to **CHECK** the expansion of Soviet power and influence. And hockey and lacrosse fans know that a **CHECK** is when one player blocks or impedes the movement of an opponent.

78 | FLAG
VERB—To become weak, feeble, or spiritless; to lose interest

A **FLAG**, in its most familiar sense, is a banner or emblem used to symbolize a country, state, or community. However, **FLAG** can also mean to become weak or to lose interest. Whenever the singer Beyoncé wins an award, she always thanks her parents for keeping her spirits up and never letting her enthusiasm **FLAG**. She says that her parents keep her motivation strong and her mind focused. Don't let your energy **FLAG**! Keep on learning your *Direct Hits* vocabulary!

79 | DISCRIMINATING
ADJECTIVE—Characterized by the ability to make fine distinctions; having refined taste

Is **DISCRIMINATING** a negative or a positive word? Actually, it can be both. Most people consider **DISCRIMINATING** a negative word because it refers to the act of treating a person, racial group, or minority unfairly. Surprisingly, **DISCRIMINATING** can be a positive word when it refers to someone's ability to make fine distinctions and, thus, demonstrate good taste. In the James Bond movies, Bond is a secret agent who displays **DISCRIMINATING** taste by ordering vodka martinis ("shaken, not stirred"), wearing Omega watches, and wearing stylish tuxedos.

80 | ECLIPSE
VERB—To overshadow; to outshine; to surpass

In astronomy, an **ECLIPSE** is the total or partial covering of one celestial body by another. A solar **ECLIPSE**, for example, occurs when the moon passes between the sun and the earth. **ECLIPSE**, however, can also be a verb, meaning to overshadow or surpass. Many hopeful singers dream of winning on *American Idol*, but the title alone does not determine their success. There have been numerous cases of other *Idol* finalists attaining major success and even **ECLIPSING** the success of the winners. Fourth-place finalist Chris Daughtry has **ECLIPSED** many *American Idol* winners in record sales, awards, and popularity. Seventh-place finisher Jennifer Hudson has **ECLIPSED** the success of many other *Idol* alumni through her album sales and her Oscar for her performance in *Dreamgirls*.

81 | COIN
VERB—To devise a new word or phrase

If you see the word **COIN** on a standardized test, you might first think of a penny, nickel, dime, or quarter. While **COIN** is most commonly used to refer to a small piece of money, it can also mean to create a new word or phrase. The English language is not static. New words are **COINED** or created all the time. For example, Janine Benyus is a natural sciences writer who **COINED** the word "biomimicry" to describe the art of copying nature's biological principles of design. Ms. Benyus **COINED** the term by combining the Greek "bios," meaning "life," and "mimesis," meaning "imitate." Architects in London are using biomimetic principles derived from ocean sponges to design more energy-efficient buildings.

82 | STOCK
ADJECTIVE—A stereotypical and formulaic character in a novel or film

The word **STOCK** has 13 different definitions, ranging from the merchandise in a store to a unit of ownership in a company. While test writers are aware of these different definitions, they are most interested in **STOCK** as a literary term referring to formulaic characters. Teen movies such as *Pitch Perfect, Mean Girls*, and *Superbad* all feature **STOCK** characters such as "The Perfect Girl," "The Popular Jock," and "The Awkward But Ultimately Beautiful Girl." These **STOCK** characters are easily recognizable but one-dimensional and **TRITE** (DH Core).

83 | CURRENCY
NOUN—General acceptance or use; PREVALENCE (DH Core)

What is the first thought that comes to your mind when you hear the word **CURRENCY**? Most people probably immediately think of money. However, **CURRENCY** can also refer to an idea that is becoming widespread or **PREVALENT**. For example, in his book *Quiet Strength*, Tony Dungy argues that a coach should treat his or her players with respect and avoid screaming at them. When he was Head Coach of the Indianapolis Colts, Dungy practiced what he preached. Although Dungy's view is gaining **CURRENCY**, many coaches still rely on old-fashioned **TIRADES** (DH Core) to motivate their players.

84 | BENT

NOUN—A strong tendency; a leaning; an inclination; a propensity

Have you ever said, "This nail is **BENT**; I can't use it?" For most people, the word **BENT** means twisted. However, **BENT** can also mean a strong tendency or disposition to follow a particular course of action. For example, the world-famous artist Pablo Picasso demonstrated a **BENT** toward art from an early age. According to his family, Picasso's propensity was so great that he drew before he could talk!

Michael Jackson and Wolfgang Amadeus Mozart both showed a **BENT** for music at an early age. When each was only five years old, Michael Jackson was the lead singer of Jackson Five and singing at several local gigs, while Mozart was already composing music!

The Kennedy family has had a **BENT** for public service and politics for generations. Since 1946, with the first-time election of John F. Kennedy to the House of Representatives, the Kennedy family has had a member in Congress (either a Representative or Senator) for over 64 years. More recently, Joe Kennedy III announced he hopes to follow in his great uncle's footsteps in Congress, demonstrating the family's propensity for public service.

85 | COURT

VERB—To attempt to gain the favor or support of a person or group; to woo

Most people associate the word **COURT** with a place. A **COURT** is where people play tennis or basketball. A **COURT** is also a place where justice is administered by a judge or a jury. But **COURT** can also be used as a verb. For example, when politicians run for office, they **COURT** votes. During the early 1970s, Richard Nixon **COURTED** the "Silent Majority," a group of voters who supported his Vietnam War policies and opposed the counterculture. In the 1980s, Ronald Reagan **COURTED** "Reagan Democrats," blue-collar workers who traditionally supported the Democratic Party. Today, candidates from both parties are working hard to **COURT** young voters.

86 | NEGOTIATE

VERB—To successfully travel through, around, or over an obstacle or terrain

The word **NEGOTIATE** is very familiar to students studying American history. Our national history is filled with examples of diplomats **NEGOTIATING** treaties and labor leaders **NEGOTIATING** contracts. But the word **NEGOTIATE** can also mean to successfully travel through, around, or over an obstacle or difficult terrain. For example, settlers traveling along the Oregon Trail had to **NEGOTIATE** their way across broad streams and over steep mountain passes. In the *Lord of the Rings* trilogy, Frodo, Bilbo, and Samwise had to **NEGOTIATE** a series of formidable obstacles before reaching the Crack of Doom in Mordor.

87 | TEMPER

VERB—To soften; to moderate; to MITIGATE (DH Core)

TEMPER is a word with contradictory meanings. On the one hand, **TEMPER** refers to a sudden burst of anger. On the other hand, to **TEMPER** means to soften or moderate one's emotions. In the movie *Happy Gilmore*, Happy illustrates both meanings of **TEMPER**. Happy loses his **TEMPER** on the golf course as he fights with Bob Barker and almost comes to blows with Shooter McGavin. Virginia successfully persuades Happy that he must **TEMPER** his anger. As a result, Happy defeats Shooter, wins over Virginia, and saves his grandmother's home.

88 | PEDESTRIAN

ADJECTIVE—Undistinguished; ordinary; CONVENTIONAL (DH Essential)

How can the word **PEDESTRIAN** have to do with both crosswalks and graduation speakers? **PEDESTRIANS**, or people who travel on foot, should use specially-designed crosswalks to cross busy highways. On the other hand, graduation speakers should avoid **PEDESTRIAN** statements such as "We are now beginning a new chapter in our lives" or "This is not the end but the beginning." Why do we call these age-old clichés **PEDESTRIAN**? Well, the word **PEDESTRIAN** can also mean ordinary and **CONVENTIONAL** (DH Essential). This is the meaning that you will encounter on many standardized tests!

KNOW YOUR ROOTS		
LATIN ROOT: **PED** **POD** foot	**CENTIPEDE**	a 100-footed insect
	EXPEDITE	to free one caught by the foot, remove obstacles, hasten, accelerate, facilitate
	EXPEDIENT	dispatching from the foot (literally), convenient, useful, fit, suitable for the purpose, advantageous
	EXPEDITION	a journey dispatched for a particular purpose
	IMPEDE	to hold the feet, hinder, obstruct, delay
	IMPEDIMENT	something that holds the feet, a hindrance, an obstruction
	PEDAL	an appendage to be pushed with the foot, as on a piano or bicycle
	PEDICURE	a cleaning and polishing of the toenails
	PEDIGREE	a family lineage, based on the fact that a part of a genealogical chart looks like a pied de grue, a crane's foot
	PEDESTAL	the foot or foundation support for a column, lamp, or statue
	QUADRUPED	an animal that walks on all four legs
	TRIPOD	a three-footed stool or support, as for a camera

89 | CAVALIER

*ADJECTIVE—Having an arrogant attitude or a **HAUGHTY** (DH Essential) disregard for others*

Fans of NBA basketball teams and University of Virginia athletic teams will quickly recognize the word **CAVALIER** as the nickname of the Cleveland Cavaliers and the UVA Cavaliers. The nickname makes sense. During the Middle Ages a **CAVALIER** was a gallant or chivalrous man. Would this knowledge help you on a standardized test? Unfortunately, it might mislead you. **CAVALIER** also describes an arrogant and **HAUGHTY** (DH Essential) disregard for others. The **CAVALIER** statement "Let them eat cake" is commonly attributed to the French queen, Marie Antoinette. She supposedly made this **CAVALIER** remark upon hearing that the French people had no bread to eat. Her **CAVALIER** attitude inflamed great dislike toward her and may have contributed to her trip to the guillotine. Today, a **CAVALIER** attitude won't cost you your head, but it could cost you friends.

90 | SANCTION

NOUN—An official approval or disapproval for an action

SANCTION is one of the few words in the English language that have diametrically opposite meanings. When it is used in a positive sense, **SANCTION** means official approval or permission. For example, if your school district **SANCTIONS** cell phones, then you have permission to bring them to school. But, when **SANCTION** is used in a negative sense, it means official disapproval and, thus, the risk of incurring penalties. If your school district **SANCTIONS** against cell phone use, you *don't* have permission to bring them to school.

91 | COMPROMISE

VERB—To reduce the quality or value of something; to jeopardize or place at risk

American history is filled with famous compromises in which two sides settled their differences by making concessions. This use of the word

COMPROMISE is so common that it is easy to forget that **COMPROMISE** can also mean to jeopardize the quality or value of something. For example, identity theft has **COMPROMISED** the personal information of millions of Americans. The quality of a product can be **COMPROMISED** by inferior materials. And finally, it is also possible for a cultural value to be **COMPROMISED**. Many **PUNDITS** (DH Core) believe that the values of hard work, patience, and diligence are being **COMPROMISED** by our culture's **PENCHANT** (DH Core) for instant gratification.

92 | CHANNEL
VERB—To direct or guide along a desired course

Why would the word **CHANNEL** appear on a standardized test? Everybody knows that a **CHANNEL** has to do with radio and television stations. But **CHANNEL** can also mean to direct or guide along a desired course.

As portrayed in *The Social Network*, Sean Parker, the co-founder of Napster, helped **CHANNEL** the creators of Facebook to success. In one scene, Sean Parker meets with Mark Zuckerberg and Eduardo Saverin at a club in New York City to discuss the future of their brainchild. Parker **CHANNELS** the team's efforts by encouraging Zuckerberg and friends to maintain minimal advertising on Thefacebook, to move the headquarters to the technology hotspot of California, and finally to change the name of his social network from "Thefacebook" to simply "Facebook."

93 | QUALIFY
VERB—To modify; to limit by adding exceptions or restricting conditions

You are probably familiar with the meaning of **QUALIFY** that means to earn the right to take part in a game, an office, an occupation. A swimmer wants to **QUALIFY** for the state championships, that is, to post a time that meets the **QUALIFYING** standards. But it can also mean to modify or limit something. You could **QUALIFY** an endorsement of a candidate for a job by saying, "Despite his intelligence, hard work, and cheerful nature, he was often late to work." This kind of **QUALIFICATION** makes a good statement less positive. You can also **QUALIFY** or **MITIGATE** (DH Core) a negative statement. For example, "The students found the teacher to be egocentric, strict, and demanding, but they later acknowledged that he had prepared them well for college."

94 | PERSONIFICATION, EPITOME; PARAGON; QUINTESSENCE
NOUN—A perfect example; embodiment

We encountered **PERSONIFICATION** (DH Core) as a figure of speech in which an inanimate object demonstrates human qualities. However, **PERSONIFICATION** also means a person or thing that represents or embodies a perfect example of some quality, thing, or idea. In Greek mythology the god Cupid was seen as the **PERSONIFICATION** of love.

In 1990, the South African activist Nelson Mandela emerged from 27 years in prison (for sabotage and other charges) to lead his party in the negotiations that led to a multi-racial democracy in South Africa. As president, he promoted policies to combat poverty and inequality and **PERSONIFIED** reconciliation rather than vengefulness. A **PARAGON** of statesmanship, he was awarded the 1993 Nobel Peace Prize. At the celebration of Mandela's 90th birthday, Celebration Coordinator George Ngwane said, "Mandela is the **EPITOME** of struggle and aspiration of humanity."

Though she died in 1996, Barbara Jordan, the first African-American congresswoman from the South, is still admired and acclaimed as the **QUINTESSENCE** of a stateswoman. She was a freshman member of the Judiciary Committee that considered articles of impeachment against President Richard M. Nixon. After explaining the reasoning behind her support of each of the five articles of impeachment, Jordan said that if her fellow committee members did not find the evidence compelling enough, "then perhaps the 18th-century Constitution should be abandoned to a 20th-century paper shredder." Beth Rogers, in her book about Jordan, writes about her impact during the Watergate scandal: "Her riveting testimony in 1974, when she **JUXTAPOSED** (Word 220) the intent and words of the Constitution against the behavior of the President of the United States, earned her America's trust."

CHAPTER 3 REVIEW

Complete each word box. The answer key is on page 140.

Gravity:

Primary definition: _____

Secondary definition: _____

Bent:

Primary definition: _____

Secondary definition: _____

Eclipse:

Primary definition in your own words: _____

_____

Secondary definition in your own words: _____

_____

Court:

Primary definition in your own words: _____

_____

Secondary definition in your own words: _____

_____

Negotiate:
List 3 synonyms: _____

Currency:
List 3 synonyms: _____

Flag:
List 3 synonyms: _____

Temper:
List 3 synonyms: _____

Pedestrian:
Use the word in a sentence that helps explain what it means.

_____

_____

Sanction:
Use the word in a sentence that helps explain what it means.

_____

_____

CHAPTER 4

Advanced Words I

Do you know what **DILATORY** (Word 139), **CAPITULATE** (Word 127), and **BURGEON** (Word 117) mean? If so, congratulations! If not, don't be upset. These words are the toughest vocabulary found on standardized tests like the SAT and ACT and on AP exams.

The next two chapters focus on the most challenging words. Don't be surprised if more than one of these comes up on the GRE, GMAT, or LSAT. Knowing the meanings of these words will significantly raise your test score by helping you infuse great vocabulary into your essay, understand difficult critical reading passages, and master challenging sentence completion questions. Don't be **DILATORY**. There is no reason to **CAPITULATE**. Study these words, and you will experience the pleasure of a **BURGEONING** vocabulary and rising test scores!

95 | LAMBASTE

VERB–Denounce; strongly criticize

U.S. financial institutions have been widely **LAMBASTED** by investors for the excessive compensation paid to the financial executives while delivering minuscule financial returns to investors. The **EXORBITANT** (DH Core) bonuses paid to the executives aroused the anger of middle-class workers whose household incomes dropped during the same time period.

Hoping to secure the votes of this large **DEMOGRAPHIC** (Word 218) group, politicians have denounced these excesses, vilifying the executives and claiming that their platform will benefit the middle class. By exploiting income **DISPARITIES** (DH Core), the politicians have **EXACERBATED** (Word 62) the already highly **POLARIZED** (DH Core) political environment in the United States. As they routinely **LAMBASTE** each other with negative advertising filled with **ACERBIC** (DH Core) accusations, these politicians have left very little common ground on which to build **CONSENSUS** (Word 54).

96 | QUIESCENT

ADJECTIVE–Marked by inactivity; in a state of quiet repose

In AD 79, Pompeii was a prosperous Roman town of 10,000 to 20,000 people. Pompeians planted vineyards and grazed their sheep on the slopes of nearby Mt. Vesuvius. The mountain appeared to be benign and **QUIESCENT**, but looks were deceiving. On August 24, AD 79, Mt. Vesuvius erupted, transforming Pompeii from a lively, crowded city into a ghost town. Modern geologists now know that Mt. Vesuvius is far from **QUIESCENT**. Since three million people now live close to it, it is one of the most potentially dangerous volcanoes in the world.

97 | PROVISIONAL

ADJECTIVE–Tentative; temporary; for the time being

In many states teenagers receive a **PROVISIONAL** driver's license at age 15 after passing a computerized multiple-choice test. The license is only temporary. After a year of driving under the supervision of an adult, teenagers may return to the license bureau to take an actual driving test with an authorized official. If they pass the test, they receive permanent driver's licenses.

98 │ LURID
ADJECTIVE—Sensational; shocking; ghastly

During the late 1890s, newspaper publishers, led by William Randolph Hearst and Joseph Pulitzer, attempted to outdo each other with sensational headlines and **LURID** stories about alleged atrocities in Cuba. For example, Hearst's *Journal American* published a **LURID** sketch depicting the disrobing and searching of an American woman by Spanish officials.

The phrase "yellow journalism" was **COINED** (Word 81) to describe tactics employed in the heated competition between the publishers; tactics that became permanent practices of journalists around the world. News events about members of the British Royal Family create even more sensational headlines and **LURID** scandal-mongering.

99 │ TRUCULENT, PUGNACIOUS, BELLIGERENT
ADJECTIVE—Defiantly aggressive; eager to fight

On February 15, 1898, the battleship *Maine* mysteriously blew up, causing the loss of 200 sailors in Havana harbor. Led by Theodore Roosevelt, **TRUCULENT** Americans demanded that President McKinley declare war against Spain. When the cautious president delayed, the **PUGNACIOUS** Roosevelt reportedly snarled that McKinley had "the backbone of a chocolate éclair." TR's **BELLIGERENT** attitude left no leeway for President McKinley to compromise.

KNOW YOUR ROOTS

LATIN ROOT:	BELLICOSE	fond of war, disposed to quarrel or fight
BELLI | war	ANTEBELLUM	before the war, specifically the American Civil War
	BELLATRIX	In ancient Rome a bellatrix was a female warrior. Harry Potter fans will recognize bellum in the name Bellatrix Lestrange.
	REBELLION	a renewed war (literally), a defiance of authority or government

100 | PROPITIATE

VERB—To appease; to conciliate; to regain the favor or goodwill of

Stung by Roosevelt's barb (see Word 99) and shaken by the public's demand for revenge, President McKinley recognized the inevitable and **PROPITIATED** both Roosevelt and the public. On April 11, 1898, McKinley sent a war message to Congress urging armed intervention against Spain to avenge the sinking of the *Maine* and to free oppressed Cubans. The Spanish-American War lasted six months and ended with the signing of the Treaty of Paris.

101 | ÉLAN

NOUN—A vigorous spirit; great enthusiasm

A leader of unbounded energy, Theodore Roosevelt promptly formed a volunteer regiment nicknamed the "Rough Riders" to spearhead the American invasion of Cuba during the Spanish-American War. The Rough Riders included an **ECLECTIC** (Word 185) mix of cowboys, Ivy League graduates, and star athletes. Although short on discipline, the Rough Riders were long on **ÉLAN**. Dressed in a uniform custom-made by Brooks Brothers, TR demonstrated both courage and **ÉLAN** as he led a victorious charge up San Juan Hill.

102 | PERFUNCTORY

ADJECTIVE—In a spiritless, mechanical, and routine manner

In his iconic song *Kiss*, Prince sings "You don't have to be rich to be my girl. You don't have to be cool to rule my world. Ain't no particular sign I'm more compatible with. I just want your extra time and your kiss." So what is the difference between a passionate kiss that proves she loves you and a **PERFUNCTORY** kiss that suggests she doesn't? A passionate kiss is filled with emotion and feeling. In contrast, a **PERFUNCTORY** kiss is a quick routine peck on the cheek. A **PERFUNCTORY** kiss probably means that a relationship is becoming routine and **TEPID** (Word 210).

103 | APLOMB

NOUN—Self-assurance; confident composure; admirable poise under pressure

On March 4, 1933, over 100,000 Americans gathered around the Capitol building to hear Franklin D. Roosevelt's Inaugural Address. The national mood was as bleak as the grey clouds on that cold Saturday. Faced with plummeting employment, falling stock prices, and collapsing banks, the government seemed paralyzed. But FDR was **UNDAUNTED** (DH Core). With his characteristic **APLOMB**, Roosevelt proclaimed: "The only thing we have to fear is fear itself." The President's **APLOMB** lifted the nation's spirit. Witnesses reported that at the end of FDR's speech, the applause was thunderous, rolling like waves across Washington, D.C.

104 | OPAQUE

ADJECTIVE—Hard to understand; impenetrably dense and obscure

The following describes a painting entitled *October* by the modern American artist Kenneth Noland:

"*The prototypical Circles, numbering some 175 examples, alone embrace a multitude of moods and means—from propulsive versus sun-drenched hues to those of the type of October, displaying an economy, coolness, and quiddity that almost anticipate a Minimalist aesthetic.***"**

Do you understand what the author is trying to say? Is the writer **LUCID** (DH Essential) or **OPAQUE**? Most editors would probably revise or delete this dense sentence because its **OPACITY** makes it incomprehensible for all but the most knowledgeable readers.

105 | CRAVEN, BASE
ADJECTIVE—Cowardly; contemptibly faint-hearted

The **BASE** behavior of the coaches of the New Orleans Saints football team was roundly **DECRIED** (DH Core) by football fans and punished by the NFL. Even after learning of a prearranged plan to intentionally injure opposing players, the **CRAVEN** coaches chose to preserve their reputations and did nothing to stop it.

When Dorothy, Tin Man, and Scarecrow first encounter the Cowardly Lion, he growls and tries to pick a fight. When he turns on Toto, Dorothy smacks him in the nose and accuses him of being a coward for picking on people and animals smaller than he is. Crying, the Cowardly Lion admits that he is indeed **CRAVEN**. He confesses that he even scares himself and that he hasn't slept in weeks because of his fears. He isn't even able to count sheep to help him doze off because he's afraid of them, too!

106 | VENAL
ADJECTIVE—Corrupt; dishonest; open to bribery

Gerald Garson, a **VENAL** former New York Supreme Court Justice, served a prison term from June 2007 to December 2009 for accepting bribes to manipulate the outcomes of divorce proceedings. Garson's acts of **MALFEASANCE** (Word 71) also involved other **VENAL** accomplices. A "fixer" would first find a suitable client and claim to be able to steer the case to a sympathetic judge. The fixer then referred the client to a corrupt lawyer who bribed Garson with drinks, meals, and money to receive favorable treatment. The fixer would then bribe court employees to assign the client's case to Garson, who would rule in favor of the lawyer.

107 | LICENTIOUS, DISSOLUTE, DEBAUCHED
ADJECTIVE—Immoral; offensive

In his book *The Twelve Caesars*, the Roman historian Suetonious described the **LICENTIOUS** behavior of the first Roman emperors. He particularly **DECRIED** (DH Core) the **DISSOLUTE** antics of Emperor Caligula. When Caligula's grandmother, Antonia, **ADMONISHED** (DH Essential) him to change his ways, Caligula rebuked her with the remark, "Remember that I have the right to do anything to anybody." Drunk with power, Caligula bathed in perfume, built great pleasure barges, and demanded that he be worshipped as a god. Caligula's **LICENTIOUS** reign came to an abrupt end when one of his guards killed him in a secret passage of the palace. At first, many Romans hesitated to believe the news, fearing that this was a trick of the **DISSOLUTE** emperor to discover who would rejoice at his death.

108 | NOXIOUS
ADJECTIVE—Harmful to physical, mental, or moral health;
PERNICIOUS (Word 204)

North Korea's punitive policies and repressive political system are **NOXIOUS** to its citizens' physical and moral well-being. Millions of North Koreans are on the brink of starvation and death because of the **PERNICIOUS** (Word 204) values of the government. The supreme leader indulges his own **LAVISH** (DH Essential) lifestyle before considering the health and basic needs of his people. Meanwhile, North Korea is a **NOXIOUS** dictatorship where thousands of its citizens are imprisoned for "crimes" ranging from "spying" for the west to not showing the required amount of enthusiasm for the supreme leader.

109 | SUPERFLUOUS, EXTRANEOUS
ADJECTIVE—Unnecessary; extra

The movie *The Dark Knight* includes a scene in which Batman leaves Gotham City and travels to Hong Kong, marking the first time that

Batman has ever left Gotham. While some critics and fans praised this **UNPRECEDENTED** (Word 70) dramatic development, others criticized it as a **SUPERFLUOUS** subplot. One movie critic called it a "pointless jaunt" in an otherwise brilliant movie. What is your opinion? Do you think the Hong Kong scenes were essential to the story or **EXTRANEOUS** scenes that should have been deleted?

Most likely the last time you purchased or rented a DVD or Blu-ray Disc, you saw a menu option for "Special Features" or "Extras." Extras or bonus features are excerpts that the director decided to share with the public to enhance the movie experience. These **EXTRANEOUS** features can include outtakes, bloopers, deleted scenes, alternate endings, interviews, or director's cuts.

KNOW YOUR PREFIXES

LATIN PREFIX: **SUPER,** **SUPRA**	over, above, greater in quality		
		SUPERCILIOUS	overbearing, proud, **HAUGHTY** (DH Essential)
		SUPERFICIAL (DH Essential)	on the surface, shallow
		SUPERLATIVE	the best, in the highest degree
		SUPERNATURAL	above and beyond all nature
		SUPERSEDE	to take the place of, to SUPPLANT

110 | DUPLICITOUS

ADJECTIVE—Deliberately deceptive in behavior or speech

Movie characters Ferris Bueller, Dewey Finn, and Frank Abangale Jr. are **DUPLICITOUS,** and all three tell lies with great **PANACHE** (Word 25) or flair. Ferris dines at an expensive restaurant while pretending to be Abe Fromer, a Chicago sausage king. Dewey impersonates Ned so that he can take a job as a substitute teacher at a prestigious elementary school. And the 18-year-old Frank convinces Brenda that he is a Harvard graduate, a doctor, and a Lutheran.

111 | PROFLIGATE

ADJECTIVE—Wasteful; squandering time and money by living for the moment

In 2011, Jay-Z and Kanye West, two of the most **PROLIFIC** (Word 166) hip hop artists, collaborated on an album that celebrates their **AFFLUENCE** (Word 42) and success. *Watch the Throne* details the **PROFLIGATE** habits of Jay-Z and Kanye, who boast about spending their stacks of cash on **OPULENT** (DH Essential) parties, couture clothing, and **EXORBITANT** (DH Core) automobiles. In their hit song "Otis," Jay-Z brags that he "invented swag" and travels in his private jet, and Kanye **ENUMERATES** (DH Core) his expensive cars, which include three Mercedes-Benzes and a Maybach. The **PROFLIGATE** rappers frequently refer to themselves as "The Throne" and, likewise, enjoy spending money like royalty.

The 20-something daughters of billionaire Bernie Ecclestone of Formula One racing fame have brought new meaning to the words "**PROFLIGATE** spending." Tamara Ecclestone purchased a Kensington mansion across the street from Prince William and Duchess Catherine for an estimated £88 million. Her younger sister Petra purchased Spelling Manor in Beverly Hills for $86 million. Both sisters did **EXORBITANT** (DH Core) **RENOVATIONS** (DH Core). The funds for the real estate purchases came from a £3 billion trust fund that Bernie Ecclestone set up for his daughters. Bernie has accused his daughters of squandering the money he set aside to provide for his future grandchildren.

112 | EPIPHANY

NOUN—A sudden, intuitive perception of or insight into the reality or essential meaning of something

One of the most significant scientific **EPIPHANIES** is Sir Isaac Newton's sudden insight that the gravitational force that causes an apple to fall is no different from the gravitational force that causes the moon to orbit around the Earth. This led to Newton's Law of Universal Gravitation. The **APOCRYPHAL** (Word 129) story of Sir Isaac Newton suddenly gaining this insight when an apple fell on his head is one of the most famous in the history of science.

In Lois Lowry's book *The Giver*, the main character, Jonas, has an **EPIPHANY** when he is made Keeper of Memories and realizes that everything is not as it seems in his seemingly **IDYLLIC** (Word 134) community.

113 | INSIDIOUS, INJURIOUS
ADJECTIVE—Causing harm in a SUBTLE (DH Core) or stealthy manner

In *The Scarlet Letter*, Roger Chillingworth is Hester Prynne's long-absent husband. He returns to Boston to find that Hester has had an affair with an unknown man and is now the mother of an illegitimate daughter. Wanting retribution, Chillingworth vows to find and then psychologically torture Hester's secret lover. Sensing a hidden guilt, Chillingworth soon launches an **INSIDIOUS** plan to torment the Reverend Arthur Dimmesdale.

114 | VACUOUS, INANE, VAPID
ADJECTIVE—Empty; lacking serious purpose

On the TV show *Glee*, Brittany is a **VACUOUS** cheerleader who is prone to making **INANE** comments. For example, Brittany responded to her teacher's question "What is a capital of Ohio?" by answering "O." Brittany is so **VACUOUS** that she was not allowed to graduate with her classmates, but she wasn't surprised. She said, "What did you think was going to happen to me? I have a 0.0 grade point average."

115 | HARBINGER, PORTENT, PRESAGE
NOUN—Something that FORESHADOWS (DH Core) a future event; an omen; a PROGNOSTIC (DH Core)

Recent scientific studies have confirmed that the North Pole is melting. This startling fact **PRESAGES** difficult times for polar bears and other Arctic animals that rely on sea ice to survive. It is also a **HARBINGER** of coming trouble for humans. The melting ice will raise sea levels, thus posing a threat to coastal cities and villages. Alarmed scientists are warning world leaders that these **PORTENTS** should not be ignored. They are calling for international **ACCORDS** (Word 47) to **ARREST** (Word 73) the rise in carbon dioxide emissions.

116 | BELEAGUER
VERB—To beset; to surround with problems

In the movie *Remember the Titans*, Herman Boone, a successful black football coach from North Carolina, is hired to replace the popular white coach Bill Yoast at newly integrated T.C. Williams High School in Alexandria, Virginia. Boone is immediately **BELEAGUERED** by a host of problems. Outraged by his demotion, Yoast threatens to resign. At the same time, tensions quickly erupt between black and white members of the football team. These tensions reflect the turmoil in Alexandria, where extremists resent Coach Boone and demand that he resign.

117 | BURGEON
VERB—To grow rapidly; to expand

Although **BELEAGUERED** by seemingly **INSURMOUNTABLE** (DH Core) problems, Coach Boone proves to be **RESOLUTE** (Word 144) and resourceful. He **ADROITLY** (DH Core) unifies both his coaching staff and his team. Once they learn to work together, the Titans win victory after victory. Community support soon **BURGEONS** as the town and school rally behind their victorious and unified football team.

118 | IMPERIOUS
ADJECTIVE—Domineering and arrogant; HAUGHTY (DH Essential)

Persian ruler Xerxes, English King Henry VIII, and French King Louis XIV were **IMPERIOUS** leaders. Xerxes **IMPERIOUSLY** insisted that his subjects all bow down before their god-king. Henry VIII **IMPERIOUSLY** demanded obedience from his subjects and his wives. Louis XIV

IMPERIOUSLY (but truthfully) asserted that in France, "L'État, c'est moi," meaning "The State is me."

119 | PETULANT, QUERULOUS

ADJECTIVE—Peevish; irritable; whining or complaining in a childlike way

Many elite athletes are seen as **NARCISSISTIC** (Word 158) and **PETULANT**. They appear to care exclusively about their own fame and desires while remaining **INDIFFERENT** (DH Core) to the welfare of the team. Their **QUERULOUS** attitude can undermine the ability of the team to work cohesively, and their unruly behavior can negatively impact the reputation of the entire franchise.

When shopping in a grocery store or a toy store, have you ever been startled by the sudden outburst of a nearby child throwing a tantrum and demanding a particular toy or treat? Then you have had the unpleasant experience of witnessing a **PETULANT** child resorting to screaming, kicking, and crying in an attempt to **COERCE** (Word 58) the parents into fulfilling his or her wish.

In *Charlie and the Chocolate Factory*, all of the children except Charlie are **PETULANT** because they are used to getting their way and become very **QUERULOUS** when they don't.

120 | COMPLAISANT

ADJECTIVE—Agreeable; marked by a pleasing personality; AFFABLE (DH Core); AMIABLE (DH Essential)

PRO TIP

Although **COMPLAISANT** and complacent sound alike, they are two very different words. Complacent has come to have pejorative nuances. It means over-contented, smug, and self-satisfied. In contrast, **COMPLAISANT** is derived from the prefix com, meaning "with," and the root plaisir, meaning "pleasure." So **COMPLAISANT** literally means "with pleasure" and thus describes a person who does things "with pleasure."

Giselle, the fairy tale princess in the movie *Enchanted*, exudes a natural goodness that delights both humans and animals. Her **COMPLAISANT** personality even charms **NOTORIOUSLY** (DH Essential) **PETULANT** (Word 119) New Yorkers who stop what they are doing to spontaneously sing and dance with the ever-**AFFABLE** (DH Core) princess.

121 | FAWNING, OBSEQUIOUS

VERB, ADJECTIVE—Behaving in a servile or subservient manner; SYCOPHANTIC (DH Core); overly obedient; submissive

Among the most **OBSEQUIOUS** characters in literature are Rosencrantz and Guildenstern, Hamlet's childhood acquaintances who, at King Claudius's command, attempt to learn why Hamlet is behaving strangely. They fall over themselves deferring to Hamlet, agreeing with him, **FAWNING** over him. Hamlet is not fooled by their **DUPLICITY** (Word 199).

Waylon Smithers of *The Simpsons* is the subservient assistant to Mr. Burns at Springfield Nuclear Power Plant. Smithers is constantly **FAWNING** over his boss, willing to attend to Mr. Burns's every whim and fancy. In one instance, Mr. Burns is relaxing in his hot tub while Smithers cleans his back with a sponge, when the following conversation takes place:

Mr. Burns: *Careful, Smithers, that sponge has corners, you know.*

Smithers: [**FAWNING**] *I'll go find a spherical one, sir.*

122 | OBDURATE, INTRANSIGENT

ADJECTIVE—Very stubborn; obstinate; unyieldingly persistent; inflexible; intractable

Spartan leader King Leonidas and President Woodrow Wilson were both very **OBDURATE**. In the movie *300*, Leonidas **OBDURATELY** insisted, "The battle is over when I say it is over. No surrender. No retreat." Similarly, Wilson **OBDURATELY** refused to accept any of Senator Lodge's reservations that would modify the League of Nations. The **INTRANSIGENT** Wilson insisted, "I shall consent to nothing."

123 | REDOLENT

ADJECTIVE—Having a strong specific smell; bringing to mind; suggestive of

It was evident that the eggs were old. The **REDOLENT** odor filled the air. It was so strong, that the bad egg smell made it difficult to breathe. The smell of sulfur from the rotting eggs was **REMINISCENT** (DH Essential) of a chemistry experiment gone wrong or an overflowing sewer.

124 | CHICANERY

NOUN—Deception by subterfuge; deliberate trickery and artifice

In her book, *Century of Dishonor*, Helen Hunt Jackson exposed the American government's **CHICANERY** in deliberately cheating the Native Americans by signing treaties they had no intention of honoring.

Are you familiar with a type of computer program called a Trojan horse? The name of this destructive software comes from the famous act of **CHICANERY** performed by the Greeks in the Trojan War. Today, a Trojan horse is an artifice that pretends to perform some desirable function, such as providing a new screen saver. Instead, once inside your computer, a Trojan horse will perform destructive acts of **CHICANERY**, such as stealing data, downloading malware, or crashing the hard drive.

125 | CONUNDRUM

NOUN—A difficult problem; a dilemma with no easy solution

Two of the largest corporations in technology and mobile devices are faced with a **CONUNDRUM**. Apple is Samsung's largest customer for components that are used in its iPhone, iPad, and related products. At the same time, Samsung is also one of the largest manufacturers of competitive devices to the iPhone. **CONFOUNDING** (Word 153) the relationship is the fact that Apple and Samsung are suing each other over patents relating to technological designs in the iPhone and Samsung Android devices. This clearly has created a **CONUNDRUM** for these two technological giants.

126 | SLIGHT

VERB—To treat as unimportant; to deliberately ignore; to disrespect

On April 29, 2011, as the world watched the wedding of Prince William and Kate Middleton, one very prominent royal was not in attendance at Westminster Abbey. In fact, she wasn't even invited! The Royal Family **SLIGHTED** Sarah Ferguson, Duchess of York, the former wife of Prince Andrew, by declining to invite her to her nephew's nuptials. The year before, the Duchess of York had been caught attempting to sell access to the Royal Family to a reporter. In response, she was not invited to the wedding, even though her daughters and former husband were. The Duchess of York later said she had really wanted to attend the wedding with her family and that the **SLIGHT** was really difficult to deal with.

127 | CAPITULATE

VERB—To surrender; to comply without protest

King Leonidas and General George Washington refused to **CAPITULATE** when faced with certain defeat. In the movie *300*, King Leonidas did not **CAPITULATE** to the Persians, defiantly insisting, "Spartans never surrender. Spartans never retreat." Similarly, George Washington did not **CAPITULATE** when the British and Hessians had apparently trapped his army on the Pennsylvania side of the Delaware River. **EXHORTING** (DH Core) his troops with shouts of "Victory or Death!", Washington boldly crossed the ice-filled Delaware on Christmas Eve and surprised the Hessians at Trenton.

128 | DISHEARTENING

ADJECTIVE—Very discouraging; dismaying; dispiriting

What do Samuel Tilden and Al Gore have in common? Both men were Democratic presidential candidates who won the popular vote but suffered **DISHEARTENING** defeats in the Electoral College. Tilden lost the controversial 1876 election, and Gore lost the hotly disputed 2000 election. However, both men overcame their **DISHEARTENING** defeats. Tilden became a major **BENEFACTOR** (DH Essential) of the New York Public Library, and Gore has become one of the world's foremost environmental activists.

129 | APOCRYPHAL

ADJECTIVE—Of doubtful authenticity; false

American students have long been taught that the Spanish explorer Ponce de Leon discovered Florida while searching for the Fountain of Youth. The story is **APOCRYPHAL**. While Ponce de Leon did discover Florida, there is no evidence that he was searching for the Fountain of Youth. Like other Spanish conquistadores, he was searching for gold and new lands to expand the Spanish Empire.

The Apocrypha is the name given to various writings that have been excluded from the Bible as not genuine. The Shakespeare Apocrypha is a collection of 14 plays that have been ascribed to Shakespeare over the years but have been judged doubtful.

130 | MAGISTERIAL

ADJECTIVE—Learned and authoritative

In England, a magistrate was a royal official entrusted with the administration of the laws. Magistrates naturally wanted to appear learned and authoritative, like the **QUINTESSENTIAL** (Word 94) magistrate in the movie *The Wizard of Oz*. The Munchkin mayor wants to appear **MAGISTERIAL** when he grandly welcomes Dorothy by publicly proclaiming, "As Mayor of the Munchkin City in the County of the Land of Oz, I welcome you most regally." Then he **MAGISTERIALLY** announces that the Wicked Witch is "Positively, absolutely, undeniably, and reliably dead."

131 | PLASTIC, MALLEABLE, PLIABLE

ADJECTIVE—Flexible; easily shaped, especially by outside influences or forces

The 17th-century English philosopher John Locke argued that at birth the human mind is a blank tablet (*tabula rasa*) and that, as a result, all of our ideas are shaped by experience. Locke thus believed that humans are by nature **MALLEABLE**. Modern public relations specialists have extended Locke's view to include the belief that public opinion is also highly **PLASTIC** and can, therefore, be shaped.

In the movie *Mean Girls*, the Plastics are a trio of mean-spirited teenage girls who have surrendered their individual personalities to the rule of behavior of their social clique as determined by the ringleader, Regina George. When a new student, Cady Heron, plots to infiltrate the exclusive trio, she pretends **PLIABILITY** to the rules of the Plastics in order to gain acceptance. Over time she becomes increasingly **MALLEABLE** to their **VAPID** (Word 114) and **HAUGHTY** (DH Essential) behavior. By the end of the movie, Cady realizes that she has become the very thing she had held so much in contempt and **RESOLUTELY** (Word 144) vows to make amends.

132 | CHAGRIN

NOUN—The feeling of distress caused by humiliation, failure, or embarrassment

In the movie *Anchorman*, Brian Fantana discovers to his **CHAGRIN** that his cologne is so foul-smelling that it repels Veronica and everyone else in the newsroom. In the movie *Pretty Woman*, Vivian is deeply **CHAGRINED** when **SUPERCILIOUS** (Word 189) clerks in a fashionable clothing store refuse to help her because of the way she is dressed.

133 | OBSTREPEROUS
ADJECTIVE—Noisily and stubbornly defiant; unruly; boisterous

The television program *Supernanny* features Jo Frost's amazing ability to tame even the wildest and most **OBSTREPEROUS** children. The hit reality show *Toddlers and Tiaras* focuses on young girls who compete in beauty pageants. Most of the children on the show are **OBSTREPEROUS**. They scream, cry, and yell at their parents, and several of them have even slapped their mothers. Many of the parents on the show could use help from the Supernanny to discipline their **OBSTREPEROUS** pageant girls.

134 | IDYLLIC
ADJECTIVE—Charmingly simple and carefree

People have different opinions of the perfect, relaxing vacation. Some love the **IDYLLIC** countryside with lush rolling, green hills and tall, swaying trees. Others prefer the simple lapping of waves on an **IDYLLIC** white sand beach. Each **IDYLLIC** location seems like paradise!

135 | DILAPIDATED
ADJECTIVE—In a state of disrepair; broken-down; in deplorable condition

In his autobiography *Black Boy*, Richard Wright provides a vivid description of the nightmare of living in a **DILAPIDATED** home furnished with broken furniture and filthy kitchen appliances. President Johnson's Great Society included urban renewal projects designed to rebuild **DILAPIDATED** neighborhoods like the one Richard Wright lived in.

136 | EXTEMPORIZE, IMPROVISE
VERB—To lecture or speak without notes in an impromptu way

Dr. Martin Luther King's "I Have a Dream" speech is one of the most **ACCLAIMED** (DH Core) orations in American history. Yet most people are unaware that Dr. King **EXTEMPORIZED** most of the speech. After beginning with his prepared text, Dr. King **IMPROVISED**, saying, "We will not be satisfied until justice runs down like waters and righteousness like a mighty stream." Knowing that Dr. King had **DIGRESSED** (DH Core) from his prepared text, the renowned gospel singer Mahalia Jackson urged him to continue by shouting out, "Tell 'em about the dream, Martin." Dr. King then began the **IMPROMPTU** "Dream" speech that **GALVANIZED** (Word 18) his audience and inspired the nation.

137 | MYRIAD

NOUN—Many; numerous

There are a **MYRIAD** of approaches to studying for tests. Some students enjoy creating flashcards while others prefer rereading notes and old tests. Another approach is creating study guides from notes and texts. The **MYRIAD** of options means that students can personalize study skills to best suit their individual needs.

138 | UNGAINLY

ADJECTIVE—Awkward; clumsy; NOT graceful

Jess Day (*New Girl*) is **AFFABLE** (DH Core) but **UNGAINLY**. In *New Girl*, Jess is a charming but awkward young woman who moves in with three single guys that she met through an online search after breaking up with her boyfriend. She considers denim overalls to be appropriate attire for a first date, and she frequently bursts into theme songs about herself. She is **UNGAINLY** in social situations, so her new roommates try to help her become less awkward.

139 | DILATORY

ADJECTIVE—Habitually late; tardy

With test scores, transcripts, applications, essays, and recommendation letters, there's a lot for students to keep track of during their senior year.

As they try to balance their schoolwork and extracurricular activities with their college applications, they tend to be **DILATORY** when it comes to the enormous task of writing their college essays. This **DILATORY** behavior is a major **BANE** (DH Core) of college counselors, who must implore them to finish their essays in a timely manner. Even though writing college essays is a daunting task, actually submitting the applications is a **BOON** (DH Core) to students and their anxious parents, who can finally relax again. We **EXHORT** (DH Core) you not to be **DILATORY**; instead, finish up your college applications quickly!

140 | VITUPERATIVE

ADJECTIVE—Characterized by verbal abuse and bitter criticism

The 2016 presidential election will be noted in the history books for several reasons. One characteristic of the 2016 campaign is the **VITUPERATIVE** tone of some of the candidates. Donald Trump won the Republican nomination in part because of his **VITUPERATIVE** treatment of his opponents. The name-calling and verbal abuse made it difficult for some former candidates to **ENDORSE** (DH Essential) Trump. The bitter exchanges so enraged voters that protests at both Republican and Democrat rallies became more frequent.

141 | DISCORDANT

ADJECTIVE—Not in harmony; incompatible; at variance with, as in a DISCORDANT detail that doesn't fit a pattern

In *The Cornish Trilogy*, Francis Cornish is an art expert who specializes in finding **DISCORDANT** details to prove that a painting is not authentic. Cornish demonstrates his amazing powers of observation and command of **ESOTERIC** (Word 188) facts when he evaluates a painting thought to be by the 15th-century Dutch master Hubert van Eyck. The painting includes a monkey hanging by its tail from the bars of Hell. This seemingly **INNOCUOUS** (DH Core) image proves to be a **DISCORDANT** detail. Monkeys with prehensile tails did not exist in Europe until the 16th century. Since van Eyck died in 1426, the painting has to be a forgery!

142 | PERFIDY

NOUN—Deliberate breach of faith or trust; disloyalty

PERFIDIOUS

ADJECTIVE—Treacherous; traitorous; deceitful; faithless

In 2012, Paolo Gabriele, the 45-year-old former butler to Pope Benedict XVI, was charged with being the mole at the heart of a Vatican leaks scandal. Gabriele was accused of stealing letters and turning them over to the press. The letters revealed an unflattering picture of corruption, favoritism shown to friends without regard to qualifications, and palace intrigue. His **PERFIDY** in taking the documents, he said, was inspired by the Holy Spirit in order to shed light on what he called "evil in the church." Even Gabriele's own lawyer has basically conceded "The butler did it!"

Judas Iscariot, Ephialtes, and Benedict Arnold were **PERFIDIOUS** traitors and opportunists. Judas betrayed Christ, Ephialtes betrayed the Spartans, and Benedict Arnold betrayed the Colonial Army.

KNOW YOUR ROOTS		
LATIN ROOT:	**CONFIDANT**	one to whom secrets are entrusted
FID | faith, trust	**CONFIDENT**	having faith in oneself, self-reliant, sure
	DIFFIDENT	lacking self-confidence, unduly timid, shy
	FIDELITY	faithfulness to a trust or vow
	INFIDELITY	unfaithfulness to a trust or vow
	INFIDEL	one who does not accept a particular faith, an unbeliever
	CONFIDENTIAL	communicated in trust, secret, private
	PERFIDY	deliberate breach of faith or trust, disloyalty

143 | PROLIFERATE
VERB—To increase rapidly

Pop and rap have traditionally been separate musical genres. But that dichotomy is disappearing. There is now a **PROLIFERATION** of songs that blend rapping and singing. Often, singers will collaborate with rappers on their songs. For example, Selena Gomez's hit "Good for You" features A$AP Rocky, and "Work" by Rihanna features Drake. There is also a **PROLIFERATION** of artists who are talented at both singing and rapping. Ke$ha has created her signature combination of singing and rapping, and rapper Nicki Minaj displays her incredible vocal range on her hit song "Super Bass."

144 | INDOMITABLE, RESOLUTE
ADJECTIVE—Very determined; unwavering

After the 2012 season, the Indianapolis Colts released future Hall of Fame quarterback Peyton Manning due to a neck injury. Many believed it was the end of the road for one of the league's greats; however, Manning remained **RESOLUTE**. His **INDOMITABLE** work ethic earned him a spot on the Denver Broncos, where he broke the single-season touchdown and passing yard records in 2013, a season where he also won the MVP award. He finally retired after the 2015/16 NFL season, one where he capped off his legendary career with a final Super Bowl victory against the odds-on favorite Carolina Panthers.

145 | MORIBUND
*NOUN—Approaching death; about to become **OBSOLETE** (DH Core)*

PRO TIP

The Latin noun *mors*, meaning "death" is also seen in **MOROSE** (DH Core) and **MORBID**, both of which mean depressed and preoccupied with death. A person who is **MORTIFIED** is figuratively "dying from embarrassment." Lord Voldemort's name means "flight from death."

As the year AD 476 began, the once invincible Roman Empire was a **MORIBUND** remnant of its once-great self. Germanic tribes overran its western provinces, while the Ostrogoths invaded Italy. After Rome was sacked by the Vandals in AD 455, the city's broken aqueducts, shattered monuments, and looted temples were mere shadows of their former glory. The last Roman emperor was a 14-year-old boy whose name, Romulus Augustulus, recalled 1000 years of past grandeur. Recognizing that the emperor was powerless and that his empire was **MORIBUND**, a barbarian general named Odoacer dismissed the boy emperor, thus finalizing "the fall of the Roman Empire."

146 | NUANCE
*ADJECTIVE—A **SUBTLE** (DH Core) shade of meaning or feeling; a slight degree of difference*

Game of Thrones is filled with characters that have ulterior motives and secret agendas. No character is as **NUANCED** in their manipulation of others as Lord Baelish. He utilizes his ownership of a brothel in King's Landing to learn and trade secrets as well as amass wealth. His incredible ambition and network of allies makes Lord Baelish a quietly powerful man in the world of *Game of Thrones*.

147 | FLIPPANT, FACETIOUS
ADJECTIVE—Treating serious matters with lighthearted humor or lack of respect

Mark Twain is famous for his **WRY** (DH Core) wit and humorous perspectives on various situations. His masterpiece, *The Adventures of Huckleberry Finn,* opens with this clever epigraph: "Persons attempting to find a motive in this narrative will be prosecuted; persons attempting to find a moral in it will be banished; persons attempting to find a plot in it will be shot." The **FACETIOUS** epigraph informs the reader that there will, in fact, be serious issues and lessons in the novel.

148 | CREDULOUS

*ADJECTIVE—Easily convinced; tending to believe too readily; **GULLIBLE** (DH Core)*

INCREDULOUS

*ADJECTIVE—Disbelieving, **SKEPTICAL** (DH Essential)*

In his famous *Histories*, the ancient Greek historian Herodotus set out to record "wondrous deeds and wars." Herodotus enlivened his pages with fascinating **ANECDOTES** (DH Core) and illustrations. However, Herodotus was at times overly **CREDULOUS**. For example, he readily accepted reports of giant ants that hoarded gold. Although normally not known for being **CREDULOUS**, Alexander the Great conducted a **FUTILE** (DH Core) search in India for the "gold-digging" ants and their treasure-filled anthills.

In another **ANECDOTE** (DH Core), Herodotus claimed that, for the second invasion of Greece, Xerxes had 2.5 million military personnel accompanied by an equal number of support personnel. Modern historians have been **INCREDULOUS** at the numbers given by Herodotus. Most have attributed the numbers to miscalculation or exaggeration by the victors.

149 | FLORID

*ADJECTIVE—Flowery in style; very **ORNATE** (Word 182)*

Romance novels are well known for their **FLORID** prose. Stephanie Meyer's *Twilight* is a popular vampire-romance novel that features **FLORID** descriptions. Here is a particularly **FLORID** portrait of Edward Cullen: "He lay perfectly still in the grass, his shirt open over his sculpted, incandescent chest, his **SCINTILLATING** (Word 201) arms bare. His glistening, pale lavender lids were shut, though of course he didn't sleep." When Edward opened his eyes, he looked at Bella "with a **WISTFUL** (DH Core) expression. The golden eyes held mine, and I lost my train of thought."

150 | EXCORIATING, SCATHING

VERB, ADJECTIVE—Expressing strong disapproval; condemning; loudly DECRYING (DH Core)

On July 8, 2010, LeBron James used a nationally televised interview to announce his decision to leave the Cleveland Cavaliers and play basketball for the Miami Heat. Cavaliers owner Dan Gilbert issued a **SCATHING** statement, **EXCORIATING** James for his "cowardly betrayal." All the bad feelings from Cleveland fans disappeared once LeBron returned to play for the Cavaliers in 2014. For the first time in 52 years, Cleveland celebrated a championship team when LeBron and the Cavaliers won the 2016 NBA title.

151 | INTERLOPER

NOUN—An intruder; a gatecrasher

In the movie *Wedding Crashers*, Owen Wilson and Vince Vaughn star as a pair of Washington divorce mediators who spend their spring weekends crashing weddings. The two charming **INTERLOPERS** always concoct clever back stories to deceive inquisitive guests. After a successful season, the pair of **INTERLOPERS** infiltrate a particularly **LAVISH** (DH Essential) wedding where Owen unexpectedly falls for one of the bridesmaids.

152 | CEREBRAL

ADJECTIVE—Intellectual rather than emotional

VISCERAL

ADJECTIVE—Instinctive rather than rational

PRO TIP

The words **CEREBRAL** and **VISCERAL** are both derived from parts of the human body. The cerebrum is the main part of the human brain and is associated with thought. Viscera are soft internal organs and thus are associated with internal or "gut" feelings.

Do you typically follow your head or your heart? If you follow your head, you have a **CEREBRAL** or intellectual response to problems. In contrast, if you follow your heart, then you have a **VISCERAL** or emotional response to problems. The *Star Trek* movies vividly depict this age-old duality. Spock is a **CEREBRAL** science officer whose decisions are governed by logic. In contrast, Dr. McCoy is a physician whose decisions are often affected by his **VISCERAL** reactions to a situation.

153 | NONPLUSSED, CONFOUNDED
*NOUN–Utterly **PERPLEXED** (Word 171); completely puzzled; totally bewildered*

On July 14, 1789, a mob successfully stormed a royal fortress in Paris known as the Bastille. The rioters overpowered the guards and seized 20,000 pounds of gunpowder. While these **MOMENTOUS** (DH Core) events were taking place, King Louis XVI spent an uneventful day hunting. The exhausted monarch returned to the palace at Versailles and went to sleep. The Duc de La Rochefoucauld-Liancourt awakened the sleepy king and reported what had happened at the Bastille. The shocking report left Louis **NONPLUSSED**. Confused and at a loss for words, Louis finally stammered, "Is this a rebellion?" The Duc replied emphatically, "No, sire, it is a revolution."

154 | IGNOMINIOUS
ADJECTIVE–Humiliating; shameful; disgraceful

2016 is turning out to be an **IGNOMINIOUS** year for the Russian athletes. It has been discovered that Russia has been running a state-sponsored doping program for decades. The findings detail a well-organized program that enabled Russian athletes to compete using performance enhancing drugs without detection. The **IGNOMINIOUS** actions of Russia's athletic federation has resulted in a ban for many of their athletes from the 2016 Olympics in Rio. Additionally, former Russian Olympic champions have been stripped of their medals as it was discovered that their victory was the result of cheating.

155 | EUPHONY

NOUN—Soothing or pleasant sounds; HARMONY (DH Core)

CACOPHONY

NOUN—Harsh, clashing, jarring, grating sounds; disharmony

> **PRO TIP**
>
> **EUPHONY** and **CACOPHONY** both include the Greek root *PHONE* meaning "sound" (like a cell phone). Since the prefix *EU* means "good," **EUPHONY** literally means "good sound." Since the prefix *KAKOS* means "bad," **CACOPHONY** means "bad sound."

In their classic Motown song, "My Girl," The Temptations tell everyone who will listen: "I've got a sweeter song than the birds in the trees. Well, I guess you'd say, what can make me feel this way? My girl, talkin' 'bout my girl." The Temptations' soothing words and harmonious melody create a **EUPHONIOUS** sound. In contrast, rapper Eminem describes his apprehension and fear before a make-or-break performance: "His palms are sweaty, knees weak, arms heavy. There's vomit on his sweater already, mom's spaghetti." Eminem's harsh grating words and rapid-fire rhythm create a **CACOPHONOUS** sound.

156 | VACILLATE, WAVER

VERB—To hesitate; to swing back and forth; to be indecisive

Hamlet is one of the best known examples in English literature of a character who **VACILLATES** over what course of action to follow ("To be, or not to be…"). And of course, many juniors and seniors **VACILLATE** over what to wear to their proms.

In most elections, undecided voters are a sought-after commodity. With a **POLARIZING** (DH Core) political process and most voters firmly entrenched in their views, the small percentage of undecided voters can determine the outcome of many elections. Bombarded by media advertising, telephone calls, and pandering solicitations, undecided voters may **VACILLATE** in their views until the "facts" convince them to support one candidate over another. Many undecided voters will **WAVER** until they are forced to make a commitment on Election Day.

157 | TIMOROUS

ADJECTIVE—Showing nervousness or fear

In the movie *Ferris Bueller's Day Off*, which celebrated its 30th anniversary in 2016, Cameron Frye is Ferris's **TIMOROUS** best friend. Cameron lacks the sheer confidence and carefree attitude of Ferris. Whereas Ferris enjoys skipping school to go on adventures, Cameron worries about the consequences. He fears getting caught by Principal Rooney and is especially **TIMOROUS** in dealing with his authoritative father. However, Cameron eventually enjoys their day off and decides to face his fears and stand up to his father.

158 | NARCISSIST

NOUN—A person with a psychological condition characterized by self-preoccupation, lack of empathy, vanity, and a feeling of self-entitlement

PRO TIP

The word comes from a Greek myth about Narcissus, a handsome youth who became captivated by his own image reflected in the waters of a pool. Unable to access the beautiful image in the water and unwilling to leave the bank, Narcissus pined away, died, and was turned into the narcissus flower, which often grows along the banks of rivers and lakes.

Critics portray Kanye West as a self-involved **NARCISSIST**, which spawned the meme 'I love you like Kanye loves Kanye'. In his album, *The Life of Pablo*, Kanye pokes fun at himself while simultaneously firing back at his critics with the song "I Love Kanye". The a capella track has verses like, "What if Kanye made a song about Kanye? Called 'I Miss the Old Kanye, man that would be so Kanye" and "And I love you like Kanye loves Kanye." This tongue-in-cheek track is meant to demonstrate Kanye's self-aware side that he does not often let the media see.

Based on a study of musical lyrics published in *The Journal of Psychology of Aesthetics, Creativity, and the Arts* by Dr. Nathan DeWall, a University of Kentucky psychology professor, egotistical lyrics in popular music reflect increasing **NARCISSISM** in our society. The study researched lyrics over a 30-year time period. DeWall stated, "What we found over time is that there's an increasing focus on 'me' and 'my' instead of 'we' and 'our' and 'us.' It reinforces this idea in American culture that we really need to focus on how people feel about themselves." [Kanye West] would be a **QUINTESSENTIAL** (Word 94) example of **NARCISSISM**, sort of feeling like you really know everything, that you know what's best; that if you don't win awards, it's not that objectively you weren't as good as other people, it's just that people don't really understand how great you are.

159 | INSOLENT, IMPUDENT
ADJECTIVE—Boldly insulting; brash; rude

Both the ancient Greek mythological character Arachne and Bart Simpson are portrayed as **INSOLENT** and **IMPUDENT**.

According to a Greek myth, Arachne was a mortal with an extraordinary gift for weaving. Filled with confidence, Arachne boldly dared to compete with Athena, the goddess of wisdom and practical skills. To punish her **INSOLENCE**, Athena turned Arachne into a spider, thus condemning her to weave for eternity.

Principal Skinner probably wishes he could turn Bart Simpson into a spider or worse. As anyone who has seen an episode of *The Simpsons* knows, Principal Skinner has had to endure Bart's **IMPUDENCE** for years.

CHAPTER 4 REVIEW

Complete each word box. The answer key is on page 141.

Flexible:

Word 1: _____

Word 2: _____

Word 3: _____

Future event; an omen:

Word 1: _____

Word 2: _____

Word 3: _____

Élan:

Definition in your own words: _____

_____

_____

Nuance:

Definition in your own words: _____

_____

_____

Narcissist:
List 3 synonyms: _____

Insolent:
List 3 synonyms: _____

Idyllic:
List 3 synonyms: _____

Myriad:
List 3 synonyms: _____

Epiphany:
Use the word in a sentence that helps explain what it means.

_____

_____

Vacillate:
Use the word in a sentence that helps explain what it means.

_____

_____

CHAPTER 5

Advanced Words II

Chapter 5 continues with the most advanced words. You'll find that we have used an **ECLECTIC** (Word 185) mix of popular and historic examples to help **ELUCIDATE** (Word 164) the meaning of each word. Don't be **CHURLISH** (Word 179), **REFRACTORY** (Word 206), and **RECALCITRANT** (DH Core). Our **SCINTILLATING** (Word 201) examples will inspire you to complete the final 68 words. When you finish, you'll be an articulate student who can write forcefully, speak eloquently, and achieve soaring scores!

160 | IDIOSYNCRASY
NOUN—A trait or mannerism that is peculiar to an individual

Red Sox designated hitter David Ortiz, photographer Richard Avedon, and football coach and commentator John Madden each has an **IDIOSYNCRASY** for which he is known.

John Madden was a professional football player, Super Bowl-winning head coach of the Oakland Raiders, and **VENERATED** (Word 214) NFL commentator from 1979 to 2008. Given the travel demands of his work, football fans know that Madden had an unfortunate **IDIOSYNCRASY**. He refused to fly! Consequently, he was forced to crisscross the country in his customized motor coach, known as the Madden Cruiser. While he was able to meet his demanding schedule in most cases, his **IDIOSYNCRASY** precluded him from covering the Pro Bowl. The Madden Cruiser could not take him to Hawaii!

Richard Avedon was one of the most famous and provocative photographers of the last century. **ICONOCLASTIC** (DH Core) in his style, he chose to reject the photography standards of his day by shooting his subjects in emotion-filled poses rather than the **SOMBER** (DH Core) portrayals that were the norm. His work ranged from fashion models to cultural celebrities to working-class people. He also continued to work in black and white when most photographers were using color. One of Avedon's **IDIOSYNCRASIES** was that, in order to create a personal bond with his subject, he allowed no one else to be in the room when he was working.

Baseball fans know that it is not unusual for players to exhibit a particular quirk or mannerism when they step up to the plate. Red Sox hitter David Ortiz's **IDIOSYNCRASY** is that he places his bat under his arm, spits into his glove, rubs his hands together, and then grabs his bat before he will take a swing.

161 | CENSORIOUS, CAPTIOUS
ADJECTIVE—Highly critical; fault-finding

In politics, running attack ads and finding many faults in your opponent(s) is a very popular method used to sway voters. This technique is called negative campaigning. **CENSORIOUS** politicians use negative campaigning to illustrate the faults of those running against them. These **CAPTIOUS** attacks have become a trademark of modern campaigns.

162 | CONSTERNATION

NOUN—A state of great dismay and confusion

In 2011, the Tōhoku earthquake and tsunami devastated Japan's eastern coast. The damage totaled over $300 billion dollars, and the loss of life was great. The tsunami was broadcast live around the world in an unprecedented news event. As the images were coming in live, the dismay and destruction in Japan was evident. Unfortunately, the tsunami was not the end of the terror for Japan. The earthquake caused the Fukushima Daiichi Nuclear Power Plant's cooling system to fail, releasing radiation eight times the normal level to surrounding areas. Japan's **CONSTERNATION** rallied many nations to assist Japan with both monetary and volunteer aid.

163 | DIDACTIC

ADJECTIVE—Tending to give instruction or advice; inclined to teach or lecture others too much; containing a political or moral lesson

Reformers of American education are advocating a move away from traditional, teacher-centered, **DIDACTIC** instruction where students are passive receptors of knowledge. They support more student-centered teaching that focuses on experimentation and discovery.

DIDACTIC literature aims to teach a moral or religious lesson. Harriet Beecher Stowe's 1852 novel, *Uncle Tom's Cabin*, traces the passage of the slave, Uncle Tom, through the hands of three owners, ending with the **INFAMOUS** (DH Essential) Simon Legree. Though the book is often viewed as a **DIDACTIC** abolitionist tract, many critics see the work as far more complex.

The word **DIDACTIC** has come to have negative connotations. Most of us find it irritating to be lectured in ways that are preachy.

164 | ELUCIDATE

VERB—To make clear or plain, especially by explanation

In the movie *Dead Poets Society*, John Keating rejects the textbook's lifeless treatment of poetry. Instead, he **ELUCIDATES** his entirely different approach by explaining, "We don't read and write poetry because it's cute. We read and write poetry because we are members of the human race. And the race is filled with passion."

KNOW YOUR ROOTS		
LATIN ROOT:	**LUCID**	lit up, clear, easily understood
LUC | to light, shine	**PELLUCID**	clear, transparent
	TRANSLUCENT	shining through, but with diffused light, partially transparent
	LUCITE	a crystal-clear synthetic resin
	LUCIFER	the Fallen Angel, who was the light-bearer to God before defying God and being cast into Hell (In Milton's *Paradise Lost*)

165 | EFFUSIVE

ADJECTIVE—Expressing excessive emotion in an unrestrained manner; gushing

Movie critics are normally restrained and hard to please. However, critics were overwhelmingly **EFFUSIVE** in their praise for Leonardo DiCaprio's work as Hugh Glass in the movie *The Revenant*. Praising his work as "an extraordinary achievement" and "one of the most captivating viewing experiences of the year". DiCaprio's incredible performance earned the actor his first Oscar, an award that had famously evaded him.

166 | PROLIFIC
ADJECTIVE—Very productive

What do the British novelist J. K. Rowling and the American rapper Lil Wayne have in common? At first glance, this may seem like an odd **JUXTAPOSITION** (Word 220). However, both Rowling and Lil Wayne are very successful, popular, and **PROLIFIC**. Rowling's seven-volume **SAGA** (DH Core) contains over 4000 pages. Lil Wayne is a prolific rapper who recorded his first hit when he was just 15. *Rolling Stone* magazine calls the rap megastar "a 24-hour-a-day recording machine."

167 | FUROR
NOUN—A general commotion; an uproar

Late into the campaign season, Bernie Sanders stirred up anti-DNC **FUROR**. Sanders's supporters, fueled by his stump speeches, became angry at the Democratic National Committee because they felt that the use of super-delegates took the power of the nomination process away from the voters. The uproar created a large fraction in the Democratic party, which many observers believed would make it difficult for the eventual nominee to **PLACATE** (Word 175) and unify.

168 | PARANOIA
NOUN—A tendency toward excessive or irrational suspiciousness; irrational fear; delusions of persecution

In *The Hunger Games* series, there is a **PERVASIVE** (DH Essential) sense of **PARANOIA** throughout Panem. President Snow is **PARANOID** about any potential uprisings or threats to his power. Thus, he kills anyone he perceives as a threat, and he imposes **DRACONIAN** (Word 1) laws upon the citizens of the 12 districts to ensure they never rebel. The harsh laws and constant surveillance create **PARANOIA** among the citizens in the districts. This overwhelming sense of **PARANOIA** causes Katniss to have difficulty trusting others when she competes in the Games.

169 | MARGINAL, PERIPHERAL

ADJECTIVE—Of secondary importance; NOT central; on the perimeter

> **PRO TIP**
>
> **MARGINAL** gives us the word **MARGINALIZE**, which means to relegate to a position of secondary or **PERIPHERAL** importance.

Politicians often speak about the importance of voting so that the people's voice will be heard. Large numbers of Americans feel that they have a **MARGINAL** influence on elections. This can be attributed to the process of electing presidents through the Electoral College. More recently, the Citizens United decision by the Supreme Court caused many voters to feel **PERIPHERAL** to the desires of corporations and super-PACS capable of raising huge amounts of money and influencing local and national elections.

170 | OBFUSCATE

VERB—To deliberately confuse; to make something so confusing that it is hard to understand

The world was shocked as details of the British tabloid *News of the World*'s phone hacking and press intrusion scandal came to light. The executives were accused of deliberate **OBFUSCATION** in their handling of the situation by insisting that only a few at the paper knew and took part in the phone-hacking and bribing of British police officers. When the situation escalated into a full-blown scandal, the respected 168-year-old paper was forced to shut down.

OBFUSCATION is also used in the world of technology. If a programmer wants to write computer applications in JavaScript but doesn't want other users to be able to read, reuse, or reverse-engineer the code, then **OBFUSCATION** can make the reverse-engineering so tedious that it's not worth the effort.

171 | FLUMMOXED

*VERB—Confused or **PERPLEXED**; utterly dumbfounded*

The television series *Lost* and the movie *The Matrix* and its sequels have complicated and **CRYPTIC** (DH Core) plots that leave many viewers **FLUMMOXED**. Millions of viewers were left frustrated and angry that the series finale of *Lost* did not answer many of the questions that had perplexed them for the entirety of the series.

You don't need complicated plots to confuse others; seemingly **INNOCUOUS** (DH Core) questions have **FLUMMOXED** veteran politicians during interviews or debates. These **GAFFES** (DH Core) leave an indelible impression on voters that have **DELETERIOUS** (DH Core) consequences on their campaigns.

172 | SPATE

NOUN—A large number or amount

Each year, moviegoers eagerly await the arrival of new blockbuster films with dazzling special effects and riveting action sequences. In the summer of 2012, Hollywood did not disappoint action-adventure fans. Studios produced a **SPATE** of popular superhero films, including *The Avengers*, *The Dark Knight Rises*, and *The Amazing Spider-Man*. Hollywood also released a **SPATE** of new installments to some of the most popular action film franchises including *Men in Black 3*, *The Bourne Legacy*, and *Prometheus*, the **AMBIGUOUS** (DH Core) prequel to the *Alien* series.

173 | INEFFABLE

ADJECTIVE—Too overwhelming to be put into words; indescribable; inexpressible

Josie (*Never Been Kissed*) and Giselle (*Enchanted*) have experienced a special and, thus, **INEFFABLE** first kiss. Josie's **INEFFABLE** moment occurred when Mr. Coulson kissed her on the pitcher's mound in front of most of the student body. Giselle's **INEFFABLE** moment occurred when she shared true love's first kiss with Prince Edward.

174 | HISTRIONIC, OVERWROUGHT

ADJECTIVE—Excessively dramatic or melodramatic; theatrical; overacted

The long-running reality show *The Bachelor* focuses on one man simultaneously dating 20 women living in the same house. This bizarre situation, coupled with a fair amount of alcohol intake, leads to **HISTRIONIC** behavior from many of the women. Crying meltdowns, slamming doors, and fights are common occurrences in each episode. The women can become **OVERWROUGHT** in an effort to win the affection of the chosen Bachelor.

175 | PLACATE

VERB—To soothe or calm; to appease

In the movie *Clueless*, Cher reacts with great **CONSTERNATION** (Word 162) when she discovers that Mr. Hall has given her a C in debate. Cher skillfully **PLACATES** her concerned father by claiming that "some teachers are trying to low-ball me." As the daughter of a high-powered lawyer, Cher views her grades as "a first offer" and promises to use them as "a jumping-off point to start negotiations." **PLACATED** by Cher's strategy, her father agrees to wait. His patience is rewarded when Cher successfully argues her way from a C to an A-.

176 | ESCHEW

VERB—To avoid; to shun; to stay clear of

The beatniks of the 1950s and the hippies of the 1960s **ESCHEWED** the **CONVENTIONAL** (DH Essential) middle-class lifestyle of their times. The beatniks **ESCHEWED** conformity and materialism. Preferring to pursue a more communal lifestyle, the hippies **ESCHEWED** commercialism and competition.

177 | STOPGAP

NOUN—A temporary solution designed to meet an urgent need

The Great Depression confronted the United States with an **UNPRE-CEDENTED** (Word 70) economic crisis. In 1933, during the famous Hundred Days, Congress responded by passing a series of emergency bills. Critics promptly attacked the National Industrial Recovery Act (NIRA), the Agricultural Adjustment Act (AAA), and other New Deal programs by calling them **STOPGAP** measures that, at best, provided only short-term relief. Historians now argue that the New Deal included both long-term reforms, such as Social Security, and **STOPGAP** programs that **MITIGATED** (DH Core) but did not end the Depression.

178 | FLOTSAM

NOUN—The floating wreckage of a ship; debris

JETSAM

NOUN—Part of a ship, its cargo or equipment that is purposefully thrown overboard or JETTISONED to lighten the load in an emergency and that sinks or is washed up on shore

In *Pirates of the Caribbean: The Curse of the Black Pearl,* Will, Elizabeth, and the crew of the Interceptor are trying to outrun Barbossa and the Black Pearl. Hoping to pick up speed and outrun the Pearl, they decide to lighten the ship by throwing goods like bottles of rum and crates of gunpowder overboard. These discarded goods are **JETSAM** left floating in the ocean near the ship.

According to legend, the Kraken was a huge, many-armed creature that could reach as high as the top of a sailing ship's main mast. In *Pirates of the Caribbean: Dead Man's Chest*, the Kraken destroys the Black Pearl, leaving only scattered **FLOTSAM** floating on the ocean's surface.

While **FLOTSAM** typically refers to floating wreckage, it can also refer to cosmic debris. For example, the asteroid Eugenia is one of thousands of bits of cosmic **FLOTSAM** in the great asteroid belt between the orbits of the planets Mars and Jupiter.

179 | CHURLISH, SULLEN, SURLY

ADJECTIVE—Ill-tempered; rude; lacking civility

> **PRO TIP**
>
> In Anglo-Saxon times a **CHURL** was the lowest-ranking freeman in the social hierarchy, the opposite of a thane or knight. These **RUSTIC** (DH Core) peasants eventually gave their label to today's rude, surly, ill-bred **CHURLS**, who can now come from any walk of life! Another word for the common man that, over time, acquired an insulting connotation is **VILLEIN**, the most common type of serf in medieval times. The meaning of the **VILLAIN** as the evil character in a novel or play dates only from 1822. Interestingly, the word **SURLY** comes from "sirly," which meant lordly, imperious, and **SUPERCILIOUS** (Word 189). Apparently anyone on the social ladder could behave badly!

Charlie Harper of *Two and A Half Men* was known for his **CHURLISH** personality. Insensitive to others' feelings, he always said whatever came into his mind. Charlie was especially **SURLY** to his mother. Take a look at this excerpt where Charlie compared his mother to The Grinch in *How The Grinch Stole Christmas*:

Charlie: *What's mom doing here?*

Alan (his brother): *Well, it is Christmas Eve, Charlie.*

Charlie: *I know. Why isn't she out stealing toys in Whoville?*

180 | RESTITUTION

NOUN—The act of making good or compensating for a loss, damage, or injury

In 1942, the U.S. Army's Western Defense Command ordered the forced evacuation of 110,000 Japanese-Americans living on the Pacific coast. Fearing that they might act as saboteurs for Japan, the government ordered Japanese–Americans to pack up their belongings and move to "relocation centers" hastily erected farther inland. It was not until 46 years later that the U.S. government officially apologized for its action and approved a **RESTITUTION** payment of $20,000 to each camp survivor.

181 | DISQUIETING

ADJECTIVE—Disturbing; upsetting; vexing; causing unease; worrisome

The 2015 terrorist attack in Paris and the 2016 attacks in Brussels, Nice, and Munich were traumatic events that horrified the areas that were affected. The ease with which known terror suspects crossed European borders, and the well-planned execution of the attacks was extremely **DISQUIETING** to all of Europe. Since these attacks, many European countries have increased security and are on heightened alert for future acts of terror.

182 | ORNATE

ADJECTIVE—Characterized by elaborate and expensive decorations; LAVISH (DH Essential)

During the 1930s, 85 million Americans a week watched a movie at their local movie palace. The **ORNATE** movie palaces boasted **LAVISH** (DH Essential) decorations and elaborate lobbies where people could escape from the hard times of the Great Depression. The "Fabulous Fox" in Atlanta, for example, featured an **ECLECTIC** (Word 185) blend of Middle Eastern decorative motifs, the second-largest theater organ in the world, and luxurious light fixtures and furniture. Today, enormous multiplexes have replaced the old **ORNATE** movie palaces. Interestingly, a grass-roots campaign led by local high school students saved The Fox. Today, the **ORNATE** building is a National Historic Landmark and a successful multi-purpose performing arts center.

183 | EXECRABLE, ODIOUS, REPUGNANT

ADJECTIVE—Detestable; repulsive; extremely bad

Third-hand smoke has an odor which is **ODIOUS**. Third-hand smoke is the nicotine residue that is left behind on furniture, walls, and carpeting after a cigarette has been smoked in a room. These **EXECRABLE** particles are so small that they can penetrate the deepest portion of the lung, a **REPUGNANT** result, especially for young children. Third-hand smoke is a recently-discovered risk of smoking. Research to determine the exact magnitude of the negative health implications is ongoing.

KNOW YOUR ROOTS

LATIN ROOT:		PUGNACIOUS	disposed to fight, quarrelsome, combative
PUGN **PUG**	fighting (from *pugnus*, a fist)	PUGILIST	a boxer, one who fights with his fists
		IMPUGN	to fight against, attack, challenge the motives of

184 | PERSPICACIOUS, PRESCIENT, DISCERNING
ADJECTIVE–Insightful, perceptive

What do the French political writer Alexis de Tocqueville and the Jedi Master Yoda have in common? Both were unusually **PERSPICACIOUS**. De Tocqueville visited the United States in 1831 and published his observations four years later. De Tocqueville **PRESCIENTLY** predicted that the debate over slavery would tear the Union apart and that the United States and Russia were destined to be rivals. Like de Tocqueville, Yoda was also an unusually **DISCERNING** observer of human nature. For example, Yoda was **PERSPICACIOUS** when he realized that the young Anakin Skywalker could be seduced by the dark side of the Force. Yoda's **PRESCIENT** insight proved accurate when Anakin became the villainous Darth Vader.

KNOW YOUR ROOTS

LATIN ROOT: **SPIC** **SPECT** look, watch, see, observe	CONSPICUOUS	open to view, attracting attention, obvious, prominent, remarkable
	INSPECT	to look at carefully, to examine critically or officially
	INTROSPECTION	looking into one's own mind, observation and analysis of oneself
	RETROSPECT	looking back on the past
	SPECTACLE	a sight, a show, a pageant, an eyeglass
	SPECULATE	to look at different aspects, to meditate, to theorize, to take part in risky business ventures
	SPECIMEN	that by which a thing is seen and recognized (literally), a sample or one individual of a group
	PROSPECT	view, scene, something hoped for, chance for success
	ASPECT	appearance to the eye, a feature

185 | ECLECTIC

ADJECTIVE—Choosing or using a variety of sources

A person with **ECLECTIC** taste in music would like Beethoven, Tony Bennett, Lady Gaga, Rihanna, Carrie Underwood, and Justin Bieber. Similarly, a teacher with an **ECLECTIC** repertoire of lesson strategies might play YouTube videos, assign Internet projects, allow students to hold debates using Twitter, and give lectures.

186 | HIATUS

NOUN—An interruption in time or continuity; a break

During the 1980s, Harrison Ford starred in three hugely successful movies featuring the adventures of Indiana Jones. After a 19-year **HIATUS**, Indy finally returned as the world's best-known archaeologist in *Indiana Jones and the Kingdom of the Crystal Skull*. Interestingly, executive producer George Lucas and director Steven Spielberg set *Crystal Skull* in 1957, exactly 19 years after the events in *Indiana Jones and the Last Crusade*. Thus, the **HIATUS** in the movies paralleled the **HIATUS** in the real world.

187 | VERTIGINOUS

*ADJECTIVE—Characterized by a feeling of whirling or spinning; suffering from dizziness; having **VERTIGO***

In August 2012, *Sight & Sound* magazine named Alfred Hitchcock's iconic 1958 film *Vertigo* the greatest film of all time. Hitchcock's masterpiece is about a retired police detective with a fear of heights who investigates the wife of an old friend and becomes involved with her. Film writer for *The Queitus*, Siobhan McKeown, says of the film, "[it gives the viewer] that **VERTIGINOUS** feeling when you can't distinguish truth from illusion. It is a film that can be watched again and again and again, always with a slightly different eye."

The Blair Witch Project and *Cloverfield* are fictional films that were presented as documentaries pieced together from amateurish footage. As a result, both films left many moviegoers feeling **VERTIGINOUS**. *Cloverfield* was edited to look as if filmed by a hand-held camera and included numerous jump-cuts that created a sense of **VERTIGO**, especially among those who sat near the screen.

188 | ESOTERIC, ARCANE
ADJECTIVE—Characterized by knowledge that is known only to a small group of specialists; obscure

Have you ever heard of the Resolute Desk located in the Oval Office of the White House? Most people know little or nothing about the desk. In the movies *National Treasure* and *National Treasure: Book of Secrets*, Benjamin Franklin Gates, a storehouse of **ESOTERIC** information, demonstrates his knowledge of **ARCANE** facts. He explains that the Resolute Desk was made of wood from the British warship HMS Resolute and then given to President Hayes by Queen Victoria. Gates further reveals his knowledge of obscure details when he explains that FDR placed a panel in front of the desk to prevent visitors from seeing his leg braces.

189 | SUPERCILIOUS
*ADJECTIVE—Showing **HAUGHTY** (DH Essential) disdain or arrogant superiority*

On *Gossip Girl*, Leighton Meester portrayed the spoiled, **NARCISSISTIC** (Word 158), and **SUPERCILIOUS** princess Blair Waldorf. Ironically, as a teenager Leighton had to endure the **HAUGHTY** (DH Essential) stares of **SUPERCILIOUS** classmates at Beverly Hills High School. The **SUPERCILIOUS** real-life 90210 students made fun of Leighton because she didn't wear designer clothes or drive an expensive car. "I wasn't very trendy," Leighton now admits. "I didn't wear makeup, and I dressed in jeans and T-shirts."

190 | BLITHE
ADJECTIVE—Joyous; sprightly; mirthful; light; vivacious

The Romantic poet Percy Shelley wrote a poem called "To a Skylark" which begins "Hail to thee, blithe Spirit!/Bird thou never wert" and which celebrates the freedom and joyous, carefree life of the soaring skylark. In the poem, Shelley likens himself, the poet, to the bird.

The British playwright Noel Coward wrote a comedy called *Blithe Spirit*, first staged in 1941 and often revived since, in which the phrase is used somewhat **IRONICALLY** (DH Core). A novelist has a **CLAIRVOYANT** (DH Core) conduct a séance which summons up the spirit of his dead first wife, who **BLITHELY** proceeds to wreak havoc with his current marriage. Eventually the second wife dies, and both wives return as spirits to cause more chaos in his life.

191 | UNDERWRITE

NOUN—To assume financial responsibility for

The Bill and Melinda Gates Foundation is the largest charitable foundation in the world. Its endowment of over $35 billion enables the foundation to **UNDERWRITE** numerous projects in the United States and around the world. For example, the Gates Millennium Scholars Fund **UNDERWRITES** a $1 billion program to provide scholarships for outstanding minority students.

192 | DISCOMFITED

NOUN—Uneasy; in a state of embarrassment

In the movie *The Princess Diaries*, Mia is a shy 10th-grade student who attends a private school in San Francisco. Mia is shocked when she discovers that she is heir to the throne of Genovia, a small European principality ruled by her grandmother, Queen Clarisse. Persuaded to attend "princess lessons," Mia feels **DISCOMFITED** as she learns the etiquette of being a princess. Mia's feelings of **DISCOMFITURE** are **EXACERBATED** (Word 62) when she attends her school's annual beach party and is embarrassed when Josh deliberately kisses her in front of a group of photographers and when Lana helps photographers take pictures of her clad only in a towel.

193 | TACITURN

ADJECTIVE—Habitually quiet; uncommunicative

Penn and Teller are famous magicians who blend magic and comedy in a spectacular performance. They began performing on stage in the 1970s and have been performing both on television and the stage ever since. The duo **JUXTAPOSES** (Word 220) each other during their performances. Penn is loud and outgoing while Teller rarely talks. Teller's **TACITURN** style accompanied by Penn's ridiculous on-stage personality adds to the comedic value of their stage performances.

194 | SINECURE

NOUN—An office or position that provides an income for little or no work

PRO TIP

The noun *sinecure* comes from the Latin *sine cura*, meaning "without care." Originally it described a paid church position that did not include caring for the souls of parishioners. That work was delegated to the parish assistant or "curate." A related word is **CURATOR**, a person who cares for a museum or art collection.

Today it is more typical for a **SINECURE** to be a payback for political contributions or for a family member who needs employment.

In the movie *Batman Begins*, Bruce Wayne is a billionaire businessman who lives in Gotham City. To the world at large, Wayne holds a **SINECURE** at Wayne Enterprises that enables him to act as an irresponsible, **SUPERFICIAL** (DH Core) playboy who lives off his family's personal fortune. Of course, this **SINECURE** and the Bruce Wayne persona are masks that enable Wayne to hide his secret identity as the caped crusader, Batman.

195 | COSMOPOLITAN

ADJECTIVE—Worldly; sophisticated; open-minded and aware of the big picture

PROVINCIAL, PAROCHIAL, INSULAR

ADJECTIVE—Limited in perspective; narrow; restricted in scope and outlook

PRO TIP

The contrast between **COSMOPOLITAN** and **PROVINCIAL** outlooks can be traced back to their origins. **COSMOPOLITAN** is derived from the Greek words *kosmos* or "world" and *polites* or "citizen." So a **COSMOPOLITAN** person is literally a citizen of the world. In contrast, a province is an outlying part of an empire or nation, so a **PROVINCIAL** person would have a more limited perspective. **PAROCHIAL** and **INSULAR** are synonyms that refer to a narrow outlook. **PAROCHIAL** is derived from parish, a small administrative unit with just one pastor, and **INSULAR** is derived from the Latin word *insula* meaning "island."

Pretend that you are the editor of a newspaper serving a community of 75,000 people. A local middle school teacher has just been named the city's "teacher of the year." At the same time, a story has just come into your office describing changing admission standards in the nation's top universities and colleges. Which story would you place on your paper's front page? Your decision will probably depend upon whether you have a **COSMOPOLITAN** or a **PROVINCIAL** outlook. A **COSMOPOLITAN** editor would favor a "big picture" outlook and give precedence to the national story. A **PROVINCIAL** editor would favor the local story.

196 | LUGUBRIOUS

*ADJECTIVE—Sad, mournful, **MELANCHOLIC** (DH Essential)*

While **LUGUBRIOUS** is frequently used to describe sad, mournful music, it can also be used to describe **MELANCHOLY** (DH Essential) people. It is fair to say that the world of music fans was collectively **LUGUBRIOUS** at the news of Prince's untimely death. Many felt Prince was the greatest musician that ever lived. Fans gathered outside his music studio, Paisley Park, in order to mourn together. President Obama said about Prince:

" *Today, the world lost a creative icon. Michelle and I join millions of fans from around the world in mourning the sudden death of Prince. Few artists have influenced the sound and trajectory of popular music more distinctly, or touched quite so many people with their talent. As one of the most gifted and prolific musicians of our time, Prince did it all. Funk. R&B. Rock and Roll. He was a virtuoso instrumentalist, a brilliant bandleader, and an electrifying performer.* **"**

197 | FECUND
ADJECTIVE—Intellectually productive or inventive, fertile

George Lucas and J. K. Rowling have unusually **FECUND** imaginations. In his *Star Wars* **SAGA** (DH Core), George Lucas created an intergalactic empire populated by humans, alien creatures, robotic droids, Jedi Knights, and Sith Lords. J. K. Rowling's **FECUND** imagination created a secret magical world populated by wizards, witches, dragons, goblins, giants, and elves.

198 | OSTENTATIOUS
ADJECTIVE—Showy; intended to attract notice; PRETENTIOUS (DH Core)

Wearing **OSTENTATIOUS** jewelry has a long history. Egyptian pharaohs, European rulers, and Mughal sultans all enjoyed wearing **OSTENTATIOUS** jewelry. For example, Queen Elizabeth I's wardrobe included 2,000 dazzling jewel-covered gowns and a diamond-covered tiara.

The passion for wearing **OSTENTATIOUS** jewelry has not gone out of fashion. Commonly referred to as "bling," **OSTENTATIOUS** jewelry is a hallmark of hip-hop culture. For example, Rick Ross, well known for his **PRETENTIOUS** (DH Core) jewelry, purchased a chain featuring a pendant with an image of himself. The eye-catching piece includes Big Boss's trademark shades and reportedly cost $200,000.

199 | GUILE

NOUN–Treacherous cunning; skillful deceit; DUPLICITY (Word 110)

What do Supreme Chancellor Palpatine (*Star Wars: Episode III–Revenge of the Sith*), King Edward I (*Braveheart*), and Cher (*Clueless*) all have in common? They all use **GUILE** to achieve their goals. Supreme Chancellor Palpatine uses **GUILE** to deceive Anakin and convince him to become his new apprentice, Darth Vader. King Edward I uses **GUILE** to capture William Wallace, and Cher uses **GUILE** to trick Mr. Hall into falling in love with Ms. Guise so that he will be blissfully happy and, thus, raise everyone's grades. Her clever ruse worked and Mr. Hall and Ms. Guise fell in love and got married.

200 | SANGUINE

ADJECTIVE–Cheerfully confident; optimistic

NASA's Space Transportation System, the United States government's official vehicle launch program, began in 1981. The program sponsored 135 flights over a total of more than 1300 days. The final launch of the shuttle program took place on July 8, 2011, as the program was **CURTAILED** (DH Core) by cost-cutting mandates. However, NASA administrator Charles Bolden is still **SANGUINE**, believing there is still a future for Americans in space using other vehicles and methods:

"As a former astronaut and the current NASA Administrator," he said, "I'm here to tell you that American leadership in space will continue for at least the next half-century because we have laid the foundation for success—and failure is not an option."

201 | SCINTILLATING

ADJECTIVE–Sparkling; shining; brilliantly clever

If you want to attend the University of Chicago, you need a **SCINTILLATING**, creative imagination. The University of Chicago's supplemental application is renowned for its **PROVOCATIVE** (DH Core) essay prompts, which are submitted to the admissions office by current freshmen at the university. The admissions committee uses these prompts to encourage students to develop **SCINTILLATING** responses, in contrast to the **MUNDANE** (DH Core) or **HACKNEYED** (DH Core) essays that many admissions committees read about mission trips, community service projects, or family trips "that changed my life." Take a look at these recent essay prompts:

- What does Play-Doh™ have to do with Plato?
- If you could balance on a tightrope, over what landscape would you walk?
- How do you feel about Wednesday?
- So where is Waldo, really?

202 | PRISTINE
ADJECTIVE—Remaining in a pure state; uncorrupted by civilization

Sandwiched between Latin American giants Venezuela and Brazil, Guyana is a small country with a vital global asset. About 80 percent of the country is covered by a **PRISTINE** rainforest called the Guyana Shield. The Shield is one of only four intact **PRISTINE** rainforests left on the planet. It is home to 1,400 vertebrate species, 1,680 bird species, and some of the world's most endangered species, including the jaguar, anaconda, and giant anteater. In a groundbreaking agreement, the government of Guyana announced that, in return for development aid, it will place over one million acres of **PRISTINE** rainforest under the protection of a British-led international body.

203 | RAMPANT
ADJECTIVE—Unrestrained; unchecked

While Guyana is taking steps to protect its rainforest, the once **PRISTINE** (Word 202) Amazon rainforest is being dramatically reduced by **RAMPANT** development led by cattle ranchers and loggers. Unless this **RAMPANT** deforestation is **ARRESTED** (Word 73), the Amazon rainforest will be reduced by 40 percent in the next 20 years, resulting in the irreversible loss of thousands of species of plants and animals.

204 | PERNICIOUS

*ADJECTIVE—Highly **INJURIOUS** (Word 113); destructive; deadly*

Francisco Santos, the former Vice President of Columbia, launched an international campaign to warn people about the **PERNICIOUS** consequences of cocaine trafficking. Santos made an example of Kate Moss, the British supermodel photographed allegedly snorting cocaine. "When she snorted a line of cocaine, she put land mines in Columbia, she killed people in Columbia, she displaced people in Columbia," Santos told a concerned audience. The **PERNICIOUS** consequences of cocaine trafficking also extend to the environment. "She destroyed the environment," Santos continued. "We have lost two million hectares (about five million acres) of **PRISTINE** (Word 202) rainforest to drug trafficking."

205 | OBLIVIOUS

ADJECTIVE—Lacking conscious awareness; unmindful; unaware

A Staten Island teenager learned the meaning of **OBLIVIOUS** and **MALODOROUS** (DH Core) the hard way. While walking down a neighborhood street, she was so busy texting that she failed to notice an open manhole in front of her. The **OBLIVIOUS** high schooler suddenly fell five feet into a pool of **MALODOROUS** sewage. Fortunately, she only suffered a few minor cuts and bruises. Her accident is a **MALODOROUS** reminder that you should not be **OBLIVIOUS** to your surroundings as you focus on texting messages.

206 | REFRACTORY

*ADJECTIVE—**RECALCITRANT** (DH Core); obstinately resistant to authority; hard to manage*

Do you believe it is possible to create a utopian community? From the Puritan communities at Massachusetts Bay to the hippie communes in the 1960s, many people have tried and failed to create utopias. While there are many reasons why utopian communities have failed, the sheer **REFRACTORINESS** of human nature is a leading cause. Petty quarrels and jealous disputes provide all-too-common examples of **REFRACTORY** behavior that often undermines even the most idealistic group goals.

207 | GARRULOUS, VERBOSE, LOQUACIOUS, VOLUBLE
ADJECTIVE—Annoyingly talkative; speaking incessantly; babbling

What do Donkey in all the *Shrek* movies and Seth in *Superbad* have in common? Both are very **GARRULOUS** and **VOLUBLE**. Donkey often exasperates Shrek with his **VERBOSE** chatter. And Seth is so **LOQUACIOUS** that it is difficult to think of a time when he isn't talking.

208 | CONVIVIAL
ADJECTIVE—Sociable; fond of feasting, drinking, and good company

A popular tradition at sporting events, particularly football, is the pregame tailgate. Tailgates are made up of **CONVIVIAL** fans that come together to socialize and enjoy food and drink. SEC schools are known for **LAVISH** (DH Essential) tailgating before their football games. The tailgate ahead of the annual Georgia vs. Florida game is so enormous and full of **CONVIVIAL** activity that it has been named the "World's Largest Outdoor Cocktail Party". The event is known for the huge fan turnout, the great food, and the massive tailgating scene.

209 | BRUSQUE, CURT
ADJECTIVE—Abrupt in manner or speech; discourteously blunt

Many professional athletes are known for being **CURT** in their handling of the media. However, arguably no player has been more **BRUSQUE** during interviews than Marshawn Lynch, the former Seattle Seahawks running back. He famously told media, "I'm just here so I don't get fined," and proceeded to follow that by answering "no comment" whenever asked a question. Lynch was very blunt with the media that he had no interest in being at any press conference and simply showed up so he would not get in trouble with the league.

210 | TEPID
ADJECTIVE–Lukewarm; mild; half-hearted

The word **TEPID** originated in the Roman baths. Bathers soaked in the hot waters of the *caldarium*, took a cool dip in the *frigidarium*, and finished their day with a refreshing bath in the lukewarm waters of the *tepidarium*. **TEPID** still retains its meaning of being lukewarm or mild. It is most often used when describing lukewarm enthusiasm or praise. For example, Sony was hoping for a hit product in the highly competitive tablet computer market, but its tablets received a **TEPID** response from gadget reviewers and analysts. One analyst stated, "Consumers want tablets, but they are not prepared to pay the same amount they'd pay for an iPad for something that's not an iPad."

Other competitors have not fared much better. Amazon's Kindle Fire HD got **TEPID** reviews from gadget reviewers, and Hewlett Packard decided to drop its Touch Pad tablet only weeks after it came out because of the **TEPID** response from consumers.

211 | PROTEAN
ADJECTIVE–Readily taking on varied forms and meanings

In Greek mythology, Proteus was a sea-god who had two unique abilities. First, he was an **ORACLE** (DH Core) who could foretell the future. Second, he could change his shape to avoid being captured and forced to make predictions. Proteus still lives in the test word **PROTEAN**. Test writers often use **PROTEAN** in difficult sentence completion questions about viruses that are hard to target because of their ability to mutate. For example, the HIV virus has proven to be particularly difficult to treat because of its **PROTEAN** nature.

212 | SOLICITOUS

ADJECTIVE—Showing great care and concern; attentive

In *Harry Potter and the Sorcerer's Stone*, Vernon and Petunia Dursley grudgingly raise Harry, depriving him of love and attention. In contrast, they are very **SOLICITOUS** of their only child, Dudley. While they force Harry to sleep in a tiny closet beneath the staircase, Vernon and Petunia give the spoiled Dudley everything he wants. For example, when an irate Dudley complains that he only received 37 birthday presents, one fewer than the year before, his excessively **SOLICITOUS** parents promise to buy him two more gifts.

213 | INGENUOUS

ADJECTIVE—Free from deviousness; innocent; NAÏVE (DH Essential); GUILELESS; SINCERE (DH Core)

DISINGENUOUS

ADJECTIVE—insincere; NOT candid; NOT straightforward; calculating; oblique

> **PRO TIP**
>
> Though **INGENUOUS** in the original Latin meant freeborn, worthy of a freeman, of virtuous, noble, or honorable character, it came to mean candid, straightforward, and frank. From there it has further **MORPHED** (changed) to mean innocent and naïve. In the theater, an **INGÉNUE** is an actress who plays the part of a naïve, innocent, inexperienced young girl. The meaning of **DISINGENUOUS** has been shifting lately, too. Generally, it means "insincere" and often seems to be a synonym of cynical or calculating.

Carrie Underwood, winner of the fourth season of *American Idol*, has gone from an innocent **INGÉNUE** to become a stunning multi-platinum recording artist. Although she is now one of the most recognizable stars in Hollywood, Carrie came from a relatively **PROVINCIAL** (Word 195) background, having grown up on a farm in the rural town of Checotah, Oklahoma.

When the **NAÏVE** (DH Essential) Underwood arrived in Hollywood for the auditions, *American Idol* host, Ryan Seacrest, asked her, "Have you seen any stars?" She **INGENUOUSLY** answered, "Well, it's been pretty cloudy." Seacrest, **NONPLUSSED** (Word 153) by her **GUILELESS** (Word 199) response, clarified for Underwood that he had meant celebrities. Quickly realizing the misunderstanding, Underwood **DEFTLY** (DH Core) responded, "No, no, just you!" and smiled at the host.

On the television show *How I Met Your Mother*, Neil Patrick Harris plays a young professional named Barney Stinson. Stinson gives the impression of being an upstanding well-educated, 30-something-year-old. The always impeccably dressed Stinson's respectable appearance **BELIES** (DH Core) his **DISINGENUOUS** character. He is a womanizer and uses a **PLETHORA** (Word 41) of tricks that he refers to as "the Playbook" to pick up women. In spite of his **DUPLICITOUS** (Word 110) ways, Stinson's boyish charm keeps him in the good graces of his friend group on the show and the viewers, as well.

214 | VENERATE
VERB—To regard with great respect; to hold in high esteem

What do George Washington and Nelson Mandela have in common? Both men are **VENERATED** as statesmen who played indispensable roles in the history of their countries. Nelson Mandela is **REVERED** (DH Essential) for his long struggle against apartheid and his leadership in helping South Africa become a multi-racial democracy.

215 | CONTENTIOUS
ADJECTIVE—Quarrelsome; argumentative; likely to provoke a controversy

Many film critics rank Mel Gibson's *The Passion of the Christ* as the most controversial movie ever made. The film provoked **CONTENTIOUS** arguments between supporters, who praised its unflinching depiction of Christ's suffering, and critics, who denounced Gibson's biblical interpretations. These **CONTENTIOUS** arguments provoked a firestorm of publicity that helped the film gross $370 million.

216 | PRECLUDE

VERB—To make impossible; to rule out; to prevent

The Duke and Duchess of Cambridge have pledged that their children, Prince George and Princess Charlotte, will live as normal lives as possible. Unfortunately, royal duties **PRECLUDE** normalcy. No matter how hard the Duke and Duchess **ENDEAVOR** (DH Essential) to keep the Prince and Princess grounded in everyday activities, the **LAVISH** (DH Essential) lifestyle of the British monarchy is anything but ordinary.

217 | COMPUNCTION, CONTRITION, REMORSE, PENITENCE

NOUN—Feelings of SINCERE (DH Core) and deep regret

On June 22, 2009, Chris Brown pleaded guilty to assaulting his former girlfriend Rihanna in a February incident. Four weeks later, the R&B singer issued a video apology, saying, "What I did was inexcusable. I am very sad and very ashamed of what I've done." But was this public statement of **CONTRITION** too little and too late? Opinion polls showed that the public was evenly divided between those who believed Brown was truly **REMORSEFUL** and **PENITENT** and those who believed his statement of **COMPUNCTION** was a **DISINGENUOUS** (Word 213) attempt to revive his faltering career.

218 | DEMOGRAPHY

NOUN—The study of the characteristics of human populations

> ### PRO TIP
>
> **DEMOGRAPHY** and **DEMOGRAPHIC** have become popular words on both the SAT and AP tests. For example, AP U.S. History exams often have questions about such **DEMOGRAPHIC** characteristics as the size and movement of American population groups.

By using **DEMOGRAPHY**, marketing executives can narrow their advertising choices and make fiscally **PRUDENT** (DH Essential) spending decisions. Cable TV channels like ABC Family, The CW, and MTV target audiences between the ages of 12 and 34, gearing their programming toward this **DEMOGRAPHIC** group. Many of the programs on these networks, like *Pretty Little Liars*, *The Vampire Diaries*, and *Jersey Shore* are some of the most-watched shows by these audiences. Young adults are a **DEMOGRAPHIC** group highly prized by clothing, soft drink, and cosmetic companies. Sponsors carefully study the **DEMOGRAPHIC** characteristics of television viewers as they make multi-million dollar advertising decisions. Many of these companies advertise during the best-rated shows on ABC Family, The CW, and MTV in order to reach the **LUCRATIVE** (Word 38) young adult **DEMOGRAPHIC** market.

219 | APHORISM, AXIOM, MAXIM
NOUN—A statement universally accepted as true

Benjamin Franklin's famous *Autobiography* contains a storehouse of wise **APHORISMS**. For example, Franklin earnestly warned students that "by failing to prepare, you are preparing to fail." Franklin's **AXIOM** is still valid. Let us **EXHORT** (DH Core) you to study the words in your *Direct Hits* vocabulary books. Always remember this three-word **AXIOM**: "Vocabulary! Vocabulary! Vocabulary!"

220 | JUXTAPOSE
VERB—To place side by side or in close proximity

JUXTAPOSITION
NOUN—The position of being close together or side by side

During Super Bowl XLVI, Honda Motor Company ran a top-rated television ad entitled "Matthew's Day Off." The ad **JUXTAPOSES** scenes from the 1986 hit movie *Ferris Bueller's Day Off* with a 2012 version of the storyline. In the movie, Ferris, played by a young Matthew Broderick, pretends to be sick in order to skip school and drive around Chicago in a 1961 Ferrari 250 GT convertible. In the 2012 flash forward, we see Broderick 26 years later calling in sick and skipping work in order to drive around Chicago in his Honda CR-V. As the **JUXTAPOSITION** unfolds, **METICULOUS** (DH Core) attention is given to even the most subtle details of the original movie, making the commercial a fitting tribute to the beloved film classic.

221 | BOMBASTIC

*ADJECTIVE—**POMPOUS** (DH Core) or pretentious in speech or writing; **OSTENTATIOUSLY** (Word 198) lofty in style*

PRO TIP

BOMBAST comes from the Latin *bombax* meaning "cotton" and Greek *bombyx*, "silkworm or garment of silk," and in its original concrete usage referred to a form of stuffing made from cotton, wool, horsehair, or other loose material used to pad and shape garments—the shoulders, chest, stomach, sleeves, and even men's hose. Though never seen in public, this stuffing was essential to men's and women's clothing in the 16th century. Today the word **BOMBAST** is used more abstractly to describe another kind of padding—in speech or writing. This padded, inflated style can be described as **GRANDILOQUENT** (literally, speaking grandly) and **BOMBASTIC**.

Sheldon and Leonard portray hyper-intelligent and ultra-nerdy physicists on the hit sitcom *The Big Bang Theory*. While Leonard tries very hard to convince people he is not a nerd, Sheldon believes himself a super-genius, and he is very vocal in describing his intelligence. He frequently belittles his peers with his pretentious speech. Sheldon's **BOMBASTIC** ego is a source of great humor on the show. Here is the dialogue he and Leonard have when they meet their new charming next-door neighbor, Penny.

Leonard:	*So, tell us about you.*
Penny:	*Um, me? Okay—I'm a Sagittarius, which probably tells you way more than you need to know.*
Sheldon:	*Yes—it tells us that you participate in the mass cultural delusion that the sun's apparent position relative to arbitrarily defined constellations at the time of your birth somehow affects your personality.*
Penny:	[stares at Sheldon in utter confusion] *Participate in the what?*
Leonard:	[scrambling to save face] *I think what Sheldon is trying to say is that Sagittarius wouldn't have been our first guess.*
Penny:	*Oh.*

222 | FORBEARANCE

NOUN—Abstaining from the enforcement of a right; the act of refraining from acting on a desire or impulse

You might be interested in knowing about **FORBEARANCE** if you take out student loans to pay for college. If you face financial difficulty after graduating, then **FORBEARANCE** can save you from defaulting on the loan. **FORBEARANCE** by the lender allows you to suspend your student loan payments for a period of time, often a year.

223 | UNFETTERED

NOUN—Free of restraint of any kind; liberated

There is an ongoing debate in education over whether students should have **UNFETTERED** access to the Internet through school computers and libraries. Most schools have "Acceptable Use" policies to provide students and teachers with the most wide-ranging educational experiences possible while still protecting them from **PERNICIOUS** (Word 204) materials or sites. The procedures do not attempt to articulate all allowable or all **PROSCRIBED** (Word 224) behavior by users, leaving users ultimately responsible for their actions in accessing and using school computers and networks.

Lewis Carroll, J. K. Rowling, and J. R. R. Tolkien have all used their **UNFETTERED** imaginations to create fantasy worlds that have blurred the boundaries between adult and children's literature. All three have also had their works converted into blockbuster movies.

224 | PRESCRIBE

VERB—To require; to order; to direct

PROSCRIBE

VERB—To forbid; to prohibit; to outlaw

Even though **PRESCRIBE** and **PROSCRIBE** sound similar, be careful, because the two verbs are virtual opposites. The confusion comes from the prefix *pro*, which usually means "for" or "favoring" but in this case means "in front of." In ancient Rome, **PROSCRIBE** meant "to publish the name of a person condemned to death or banishment." Now it has come to mean "to prohibit."

During the Prohibition Era (1919 to 1933) the manufacture, sale, or transportation of alcohol was **PROSCRIBED** in the U.S. Now alcohol consumption by adults is permitted, but each state may **PRESCRIBE** its minimum drinking age. In 1984, President Ronald Reagan responded to the tragic **ANECDOTES** (DH Core) told by Mothers Against Drunk Driving (MADD) of accidents involving young people driving to states with lower drinking ages. The National Minimum Drinking Age Act pressured the states to **PROSCRIBE** the purchase and possession of alcohol by anyone under the age of 21 or lose 10 percent of their annual federal highway apportionment.

225 | PUERILE, CALLOW, SOPHOMORIC
ADJECTIVE—Childishly foolish; inexperienced; immature

The **SOPHOMORIC** movie *Superbad* is a semi-autobiographical story written by two 15-year-old boys. It depicts two **CALLOW** teenage boys who are finally invited to a party at the end of senior year by a popular female classmate. They enlist the help of their uber-nerdy friend, who is able to get a fake ID, and the boys hatch a plan to bring alcohol to the party. Their **PUERILE** antics, designed to impress the girl hosting the party and her party-crazed friends, make for a raucous night and teach some life lessons.

In *Mall Rats*, Holden's girlfriend calls him "**CALLOW**" in a letter breaking up with him. But Holden thinks "**CALLOW**" is a compliment until a friend tells him: "Dude, **CALLOW** is not good."

226 | POLYMATH

NOUN—A person whose expertise spans a significant number of subject areas

DILETTANTE

*NOUN—An amateur or dabbler; a person with a **SUPERFICIAL** (DH Core) interest in an art or a branch of knowledge; a trifler*

PRO TIP

DILETTANTE comes from the Italian, meaning a "lover of the arts" and goes back to the Latin *dilettare*, to delight.

Originally it did not carry the **PEJORATIVE** (negative) connotations that it holds today. In the 17th and 18th centuries, people were more inclined to celebrate the "well-rounded Renaissance man." Perhaps it was easier to master a number of fields when there was less to be known.

POLYMATH Benjamin Franklin (1706-1790), noted author, printer, inventor, scientist, political theorist, musician, satirist, diplomat, and statesman, had a **MYRIAD** (Word 137) of interests, all of which he developed to a remarkable degree. His diligence, intelligence, common sense, strength of character, and **TENACITY** (DH Core) helped him to become one of the most influential of the Founding Fathers.

In contrast, Max Fischer, a high school sophomore in Wes Anderson's movie *Rushmore*, is flunking every subject, but he is involved in virtually every extra-curricular activity offered at his school. The bizarre list of activities—from Beekeeping to Debate to JV Decathlon to Second Chorale Director—**SATIRIZES** (DH Core) the culture of the **DILETTANTE**, a "Jack of all trades, but master of none."

In recent years, colleges have been sending the message that they would prefer candidates who delve deeply into one or several areas of interest instead of those who pad their resumés with long lists of activities that could only have commanded **DILETTANTISH** attention.

227 | DISSEMBLER, PREVARICATOR
NOUN—A liar and deceiver

In *Mean Girls*, Regina George is a cunning **DISSEMBLER** who deliberately lies to her friends and to her enemies. In the movie *Pirates of the Caribbean: Curse of the Black Pearl*, Captain Barbossa is a **PREVARICATOR** who repeatedly lies to Jack Sparrow, Elizabeth Swann, and Will Turner.

CHAPTER 5 REVIEW

Complete each word box. The answer key is on page 141.

Ill-tempered:

Word 1: _____

Word 2: _____

Word 3: _____

Insightful:

Word 1: _____

Word 2: _____

Word 3: _____

Placate:

Definition in your own words: _____

_____

Bombastic:

Definition in your own words: _____

_____

Lugubrious:
List 3 synonyms: _____

Churlish:
List 3 synonyms: _____

Curt:
List 3 synonyms: _____

Contrition:
List 3 synonyms: _____

Fecund:
Use the word in a sentence that helps explain what it means.

_____

_____

Venerate:
Use the word in a sentence that helps explain what it means.

_____

_____

Fast Review

CHAPTER 1: EVERY WORD HAS A HISTORY

1. **DRACONIAN** *(adj.)*—Characterized by very strict laws, rules, and punishments

2. **LACONIC, SUCCINCT, TERSE** *(adj.)*—Very brief; concise

3. **SPARTAN** *(adj.)*—Plain; simple; **AUSTERE** (DH Core)

4. **HALCYON** *(adj.)*—Idyllically calm and peaceful; an untroubled golden time of satisfaction, happiness, and tranquility

5. **SOPHISTRY** *(n.)*—A plausible but deliberately misleading or **FALLACIOUS** argument designed to deceive someone

6. **CHIMERICAL** *(adj.)*—Given to fantastic schemes; existing only in the imagination; impossible; vainly conceived

7. **OSTRACIZE** *(v.)*—To deliberately exclude from a group; to **BANISH**

8. **IMPECUNIOUS** *(adj.)*—Poor; penniless; NOT **AFFLUENT** (Word 42)

9. **NEFARIOUS** *(adj.)*—Famous for being wicked; **VILLAINOUS**; vile

10. **JOVIAL, , JOCULAR** *(adj.)*—Good-humored; cheerful

11. **DIRGE** *(n.)*—A funeral hymn; a slow, mournful, **LUGUBRIOUS** (Word 196) musical composition

12. **MAUDLIN** *(adj.)*—Tearful; excessively sentimental

13. **QUIXOTIC** *(adj.)*—Foolishly impractical in the pursuit of ideals; impractical idealism

14. **PANDEMONIUM** *(n.)*—A wild uproar; tumult

15. **MARTINET** *(n.)*—A strict disciplinarian; a person who demands absolute adherence to forms and rules

16. **FIASCO** *(n.)*—A complete failure; a **DEBACLE**

17. **BOWDLERIZE** *(v.)*—To remove or delete parts of a book, song, or other work that are considered offensive; to **EXPURGATE** (DH Core)

18. **GALVANIZE** *(v.)*—To electrify; to stir into action as if with an electric shock

19. **PICAYUNE** *(adj.)*—Small value or importance; petty; trifling

20. **GERRYMANDER** *(n.)*—To divide a geographic area into voting districts so as to give unfair advantage to one party in elections

21. **MAVERICK** *(n.)*—An independent individual who does not go along with a group or party; a nonconformist

22. **JUGGERNAUT** *(n.)*—An irresistible force that crushes everything in its path

23. **SERENDIPITY** *(n.)*—Discovery by fortunate accident

24. **NADIR** *(n.)*—The lowest point; the bottom

25. **PANACHE, VERVE, FLAMBOYANCE, ÉLAN** (Word 101) *(n.)*—Great vigor and energy; dash, especially in artistic performance and composition

CHAPTER 2: SCIENCE AND THE SOCIAL SCIENCES

26. **CATALYST** *(n.)*—In chemistry, a **CATALYST** is a substance (such as an enzyme) that accelerates the rate of a chemical reaction at some temperature, but without itself being transformed or consumed by the reaction. In everyday usage a **CATALYST** is any agent that provokes or triggers change.

27. **CAUSTIC** *(adj.)*—In chemistry, a **CAUSTIC** substance is one that burns or destroys organic tissue by chemical action. Hydrofluoric acid and silver nitrate are examples of **CAUSTIC** substances. In everyday usage, a **CAUSTIC** comment is one that hurts or burns.

28. **CRYSTALLIZE** *(v.)*—In chemistry, **CRYSTALLIZATION** is the process by which crystals are formed. In everyday usage, to **CRYSTALLIZE** means to give a definite form to an idea or plan.

29. **OSMOSIS** *(n.)*—In chemistry, **OSMOSIS** refers to the diffusion of a fluid through a semi-permeable membrane until there is an equal concentration of fluid on both sides of the membrane. In everyday usage, **OSMOSIS** refers to a gradual, often unconscious process of **ASSIMILATION**.

30. **SEDENTARY** *(adj.)*—In ecology, animals that are **SEDENTARY** remain or live in one area. In everyday usage, **SEDENTARY** means settled and therefore accustomed to sitting or doing little exercise.

31. **VIRULENT** *(adj.)*—In medical science, **VIRULENT** refers to a disease or toxin that is extremely infectious, malignant, or poisonous. In everyday usage, **VIRULENT** refers to language that is bitterly hostile, hateful, and antagonistic.

32. **EMPIRICAL** *(adj.)*—In science, **EMPIRICAL** means originating in or based on direct observation and experience. **EMPIRICAL** data can then be used to support or reject a hypothesis. In everyday language, **EMPIRICAL** means to be guided by practical experience, not theory.

33. **ENTOMOLOGY** *(n.)*—The scientific study of insects

34. **GESTATE** *(v.)*—In science, **GESTATE** means to carry within the uterus from conception to delivery. In everyday language, **GESTATE** means to conceive and develop in the mind.

35. **CATHARTIC** *(adj.)*—Purgative, either physically or emotionally; cleansing

36. **PARADIGM** *(n.)*—In science, a **PARADIGM** is a framework or model of thought

37. **ENTREPRENEUR** *(n.)*—A person who organizes and manages a business or enterprise

38. **LUCRATIVE** *(adj.)*—Very profitable

39. **EXTRAVAGANT** *(adj.)*—Excessive and therefore lacking restraint

40. **AVARICE, CUPIDITY** *(n.)*—Excessive desire for material wealth; greed; **COVETOUSNESS** (DH Core)

41. **GLUT, PLETHORA, SURFEIT** *(n.)*—A surplus or excess of something

42. **DESTITUTE, IMPOVERISHED, INDIGENT** *(adj.)*—Very poor, lacking basic resources
     AFFLUENT *(adj.)*—Very rich, having abundant resources

43. **MUNIFICENT** *(adj.)*—Very generous

44. **PARSIMONIOUS** *(adj.)*—Excessively cheap with money; stingy

45. **DEPRECIATION** *(n.)*—Any decrease or loss in value caused by age, wear, or market conditions

46. **REMUNERATE** *(v.)*—To compensate; to make payment for; to pay a person

47. **ACCORD** *(n.)*—A formal concurrence, agreement, or harmony of minds

48. **ENLIGHTEN, EDIFY** *(v.)*—To inform, instruct, illuminate, remove darkness and ignorance
ERUDITE *(adj.)*—Learned, literate, or authoritative

49. **APPEASEMENT** *(n.)*—The policy of granting concessions to maintain peace

50. **NULLIFY** *(v.)*—To make null; to declare invalid

51. **TRIUMVIRATE** *(n.)*—A group or association of three leaders

52. **PRETEXT** *(n.)*—An excuse; an alleged cause

53. **WATERSHED** *(n.)*—Critical point that marks a change of course; a turning point

54. **CONSENSUS** *(n.)*—A general agreement

55. **AUTOCRAT, DESPOT** *(n.)*—A ruler or other person with unlimited power and authority

56. **MANIFESTO** *(n.)*—A public declaration of beliefs, policies, or intentions

57. **ENFRANCHISE** *(v.)*—To endow with the rights of citizenship, especially the right to vote
DISENFRANCHISE *(v.)*—To deprive of some privilege or right, especially the right to vote

58. **COERCE** *(v.)*—To force to act or think in a certain way by use of pressure, threats, or torture; to compel

59. **EGALITARIAN** *(adj.)*—Favoring social equality; believing in a society in which all people have equal political, economic, and civil rights

60. **DEMARCATION** *(n.)*—The setting or marking of boundaries or limits, as a line of demarcation

61. **INQUISITION** *(n.)*—A severe interrogation; a systematic questioning

62. **AMELIORATE** *(v.)*—To make a situation better
EXACERBATE *(v.)*—To make a situation worse

63. **DESICCATED** *(adj.)*—Thoroughly dried out; lifeless, totally arid

64. **CONTIGUOUS** *(adj.)*—Sharing an edge or boundary; touching

65. **PERTINENT** *(adj.)*—Relevant; to the point; clearly illustrative of a major point

66. **COMPLICITY** *(n.)*—Association or participation in a wrongful act

67. **EXONERATE, EXCULPATE** *(v.)*—To free from guilt or blame

68. **INDISPUTABLE** *(adj.)*—Not open to question; undeniable; irrefutable

69. **PRECEDENT** *(n.)*—An act or instance that is used as an example in dealing with subsequent similar instances; a historical **PARADIGM** (Word 36)

70. **UNPRECEDENTED** *(adj.)*—Without previous example, never known before; an **UNPRECEDENTED** event has never happened before

71. **MALFEASANCE** *(n.)*—Misconduct or wrongdoing, especially by a public official; intentionally performing an act that is illegal

72. **PROBITY** *(n.)*—Integrity and uprightness; honesty; high moral standards

CHAPTER 3: WORDS WITH MULTIPLE MEANINGS

73. **ARREST** *(v.)*—To bring to a stop; to halt

74. **GRAVITY** *(n.)*—Seriousness; dignity; solemnity; weight

75. **PRECIPITATE** *(v.)*—To cause, to bring about prematurely, hastily or suddenly; impulsive

76. **RELIEF** *(n.)*—Elevation of a land surface
    (n.)—A feeling of reassurance or relaxation

77. **CHECK** *(v.)*—To restrain; halt; hold back; contain

78. **FLAG** *(v.)*—To become weak, feeble, or spiritless; to lose interest

79. **DISCRIMINATING** *(adj.)*—Characterized by the ability to make fine distinctions; having refined taste

80. **ECLIPSE** *(v.)*—To overshadow; to outshine; to surpass

81. **COIN** *(v.)*—To devise a new word or phrase

82. **STOCK** *(adj.)*—A stereotypical and formulaic character in a novel or film

83. **CURRENCY** *(n.)*—General acceptance or use; **PREVALENCE** (DH Core)

84. **BENT** *(n.)*—A strong tendency; a leaning; an inclination; a propensity

85. **COURT** *(v.)*—To attempt to gain the favor or support of a person or group; to woo

86. **NEGOTIATE** *(v.)*—To successfully travel through, around, or over an obstacle or terrain

87. **TEMPER** *(v.)*—To soften; to moderate; to **MITIGATE** (DH Core)

88. **PEDESTRIAN** *(adj.)*—Undistinguished; ordinary; **CONVENTIONAL** (DH Essential)

89. **CAVALIER** *(adj.)*—Having an arrogant attitude or a **HAUGHTY** (DH Essential) disregard for others

90. **SANCTION** *(n.)*—An official approval or disapproval for an action

91. **COMPROMISE** *(v.)*—To reduce the quality or value of something; to jeopardize or place at risk

92. **CHANNEL** *(v.)*—To direct or guide along a desired course

93. **QUALIFY** *(v.)*—To modify; to limit by adding exceptions or restricting conditions

94. **PERSONIFICATION, EPITOME; PARAGON; QUINTESSENCE** *(n.)*—A perfect example; embodiment

CHAPTER 4: ADVANCED WORDS I

95. **LAMBASTE** *(v.)*—Denounce; strongly criticize

96. **QUIESCENT** *(adj.)*—Marked by inactivity; in a state of quiet repose

97. **PROVISIONAL** *(adj.)*—Tentative; temporary; for the time being

98. **LURID** *(adj.)*—Sensational; shocking; ghastly

99. **TRUCULENT, PUGNACIOUS, BELLIGERENT** *(adj.)*—Defiantly aggressive; eager to fight

100. **PROPITIATE** *(v.)*—To appease; to conciliate; to regain the favor or goodwill of

101. **ÉLAN** *(n.)*—A vigorous spirit; great enthusiasm

102. **PERFUNCTORY** *(adj.)*—In a spiritless, mechanical, and routine manner

103. **APLOMB** *(n.)*—Self-assurance; confident composure; admirable poise under pressure

104. **OPAQUE** *(adj.)*—Hard to understand; impenetrably dense and obscure

105. **CRAVEN, BASE** *(adj.)*—Cowardly; contemptibly faint-hearted

106. **VENAL** *(adj.)*—Corrupt; dishonest; open to bribery

107. **LICENTIOUS, DISSOLUTE, DEBAUCHED** *(adj.)*—Immoral; offensive

108. **NOXIOUS, INJURIOUS** *(adj.)*—Harmful to physical, mental, or moral health; **PERNICIOUS** (Word 204)

109. **SUPERFLUOUS, EXTRANEOUS** *(adj.)*—Unnecessary; extra

110. **DUPLICITOUS** *(adj.)*—Deliberately deceptive in behavior or speech

111. **PROFLIGATE** *(adj.)*—Wasteful; squandering time and money by living for the moment

112. **EPIPHANY** *(n.)*—A sudden realization; an insightful moment

113. **INSIDIOUS** *(adj.)*—Causing harm in a **SUBTLE** (DH Core) or stealthy manner

114. **VACUOUS, INANE, VAPID** *(adj.)*—Empty; lacking serious purpose

115. **HARBINGER, PORTENT, PRESAGE** *(n.)*—Something that **FORESHADOWS** (DH Core) a future event; an omen; a **PROGNOSTIC** (DH Core)

116. **BELEAGUER** *(v.)*—To beset; to surround with problems

117. **BURGEON** *(v.)*—To grow rapidly; to expand

118. **IMPERIOUS** *(adj.)*—Domineering and arrogant; **HAUGHTY** (DH Essential)

119. **PETULANT, QUERULOUS** *(adj.)*—Peevish; irritable; whining or complaining in a childlike way

120. **COMPLAISANT** *(adj.)*—Agreeable; marked by a pleasing personality; **AFFABLE** (DH Core); **AMIABLE** (DH Essential)

121. **FAWNING** *(v.)*, **OBSEQUIOUS** *(adj.)*—Behaving in a servile or **SUBSERVIENT** manner; **SYCOPHANTIC** (DH Core); overly obedient; submissive

122. **OBDURATE, INTRANSIGENT** *(adj.)*—Very stubborn; obstinate; unyieldingly persistent; inflexible; intractable

123. **REDOLENT** *(adj.)*—Having a strong specific smell; bringing to mind; suggestive of

124. **CHICANERY** *(n.)*—Deception by subterfuge; deliberate trickery and artifice

125. **CONUNDRUM** *(n.)*—A difficult problem; a dilemma with no easy solution

126. **SLIGHT** *(v.)*—To treat in a disparaging manner; to deliberately ignore; to disrespect

127. **CAPITULATE** *(v.)*—To surrender; to comply without protest

128. **DISHEARTENING** *(adj.)*—Very discouraging; dismaying; dispiriting

129. **APOCRYPHAL** *(adj.)*—Of doubtful authenticity; false

130. **MAGISTERIAL** *(adj.)*—Learned and authoritative

131. **PLASTIC, MALLEABLE, PLIABLE** *(adj.)*—Flexible; easily shaped, especially by outside influences or forces

132. **CHAGRIN** *(n.)*—The feeling of distress caused by humiliation, failure, or embarrassment

133. **OBSTREPEROUS** *(adj.)*—Noisily and stubbornly defiant; unruly; boisterous

134. **IDYLLIC** *(adj.)*—Charmingly simple and carefree

135. **DILAPIDATED** *(adj.)*—In a state of disrepair; broken-down; in deplorable condition

136. **EXTEMPORIZE, IMPROVISE** *(v.)*—To lecture or speak without notes in an impromptu way

137. **MYRIAD** *(n.)*—Many; numerous

138. **UNGAINLY** *(adj.)*—Awkward; clumsy; NOT graceful

139. **DILATORY** *(adj.)*—Habitually late; tardy

140. **VITUPERATIVE** *(adj.)*—Characterized by verbal abuse and bitter criticism

141. **DISCORDANT** *(adj.)*—Not in harmony; incompatible; at variance with, as in a **DISCORDANT** detail that doesn't fit a pattern

142. **PERFIDY** *(n.)*—Deliberate breach of faith or trust; disloyalty
    PERFIDIOUS *(adj.)*—Treacherous; traitorous; deceitful; faithless

143. **PROLIFERATE** *(v.)*—To increase rapidly

144. **INDOMITABLE, RESOLUTE** *(adj.)*—Very determined; unwavering

145. **MORIBUND** *(adj.)*—Approaching death; about to become **OBSOLETE** (DH Core)

146. **NUANCE** *(n.)*—A **SUBTLE** (DH Core) shade of meaning or feeling; a slight degree of difference

147. **FLIPPANT, FACETIOUS** *(adj.)*—Treating serious matters with lighthearted humor or lack of respect

148. **CREDULOUS** *(adj.)*—Easily convinced; tending to believe too readily; **GULLIBLE**
    INCREDULOUS *(adj.)*—Disbelieving, **SKEPTICAL** (DH Essential)

149. **FLORID** *(adj.)*—Flowery in style; very **ORNATE** (Word 182)

150. **EXCORIATING** *(n.)*, **SCATHING** *(adj.)*—Expressing strong disapproval; condemning; loudly **DECRYING** (DH Core)

151. **INTERLOPER** *(n.)*—An intruder; a gatecrasher

152. **CEREBRAL** *(adj.)*—Intellectual rather than emotional
    VISCERAL *(adj.)*—Instinctive rather than rational

153. **NONPLUSSED, CONFOUNDED** *(n.)*—Utterly **PERPLEXED** (Word 171); completely puzzled; totally bewildered

154. **IGNOMINIOUS** *(adj.)*—Humiliating; shameful; disgraceful

155. **EUPHONY** *(n.)*—Soothing or pleasant sounds; harmony
    CACOPHONY *(n.)*—Harsh, clashing, jarring, grating sounds; disharmony

156. **VACILLATE, WAVER** *(v.)*—To hesitate; to swing back and forth; to be indecisive

157. **TIMOROUS** *(adj.)*—Showing nervousness or fear

158. **NARCISSIST** *(n.)*—A person with a psychological condition characterized by self-preoccupation, lack of empathy, vanity, and a feeling of self-entitlement

159. **INSOLENT, IMPUDENT** *(adj.)*—Boldly insulting; brash; rude

CHAPTER 5: ADVANCED WORDS II

160. **IDIOSYNCRASY** *(n.)*—A trait or mannerism that is peculiar to an individual

161. **CENSORIOUS, CAPTIOUS** *(adj.)*—Highly critical; fault-finding

162. **CONSTERNATION** *(n.)*—A state of great dismay and confusion

163. **DIDACTIC** *(adj.)*—Tending to give instruction or advice; inclined to teach or lecture others too much; containing a political or moral lesson

164. **ELUCIDATE** *(v.)*—To make clear or plain, especially by explanation

165. **EFFUSIVE** *(adj.)*—Expressing excessive emotion in an unrestrained manner; gushing

166. **PROLIFIC** *(adj.)*—Very productive

167. **FUROR** *(n.)*—A general commotion; an uproar

168. **PARANOIA** *(n.)*—A tendency toward excessive or irrational suspiciousness; irrational fear; delusions of persecution

169. **MARGINAL, PERIPHERAL** *(adj.)*—Of secondary importance; NOT central; on the perimeter

170. **OBFUSCATE** *(v.)*—To deliberately confuse; to make something so confusing that it is hard to understand

171. **FLUMMOXED** *(v.)*—Confused or **PERPLEXED**; utterly dumbfounded

172. **SPATE** *(n.)*—A large number or amount

173. **INEFFABLE** *(adj.)*—Too overwhelming to be put into words; indescribable; inexpressible

174. **HISTRIONIC, OVERWROUGHT** *(adj.)*—Excessively dramatic or melodramatic; theatrical; overacted

175. **PLACATE** *(v.)*—To soothe or calm; to appease

176. **ESCHEW** *(v.)*—To avoid; to shun; to stay clear of

177. **STOPGAP** *(n.)*—A temporary solution designed to meet an urgent need

178. **FLOTSAM** *(n.)*—The floating wreckage of a ship; debris
JETSAM *(n.)*—Part of a ship, its cargo or equipment that is purposefully thrown overboard or **JETTISONED** to lighten the load in an emergency and that sinks or is washed up on shore

179. **CHURLISH, SULLEN, SURLY** *(adj.)*—Ill-tempered; rude; lacking civility

180. **RESTITUTION** *(n.)*—The act of making good or compensating for a loss, damage, or injury

181. **DISQUIETING** *(adj.)*—Disturbing; upsetting; vexing; causing unease; worrisome

182. **ORNATE** *(adj.)*—Characterized by elaborate and expensive decorations; **LAVISH** (DH Essential)

183. **EXECRABLE, ODIOUS, REPUGNANT** *(adj.)*—Detestable; repulsive; extremely bad

184. **PERSPICACIOUS, PRESCIENT, DISCERNING** *(adj.)*—Insightful, perceptive

185. **ECLECTIC** *(adj.)*—Choosing or using a variety of sources

186. **HIATUS** *(n.)*—An interruption in time or continuity; a break

187. **VERTIGINOUS** *(adj.)*—Characterized by or suffering from dizziness; having **VERTIGO**

188. **ESOTERIC, ARCANE** *(adj.)*—Characterized by knowledge that is known only to a small group of specialists; obscure

189. **SUPERCILIOUS** *(adj.)*—Showing **HAUGHTY** (DH Essential) disdain or arrogant superiority

190. **BLITHE** *(adj.)*—Joyous; sprightly; mirthful; light; vivacious

191. **UNDERWRITE** *(v.)*—To assume financial responsibility for

192. **DISCOMFITED** *(n.)*—Uneasy; in a state of embarrassment

193. **TACITURN** *(adj.)*—Habitually quiet; uncommunicative

194. **SINECURE** *(n.)*—An office or position that provides an income for little or no work

195. **COSMOPOLITAN** *(adj.)*—Worldly; sophisticated; open-minded and aware of the big picture
PROVINCIAL, PAROCHIAL, INSULAR *(adj.)*—Limited in perspective; narrow; restricted in scope and outlook

196. **LUGUBRIOUS** *(adj.)*—Sad, mournful, **MELANCHOLIC** (DH Essential)

197. **FECUND** *(adj.)*—Intellectually productive or inventive, fertile

198. **OSTENTATIOUS** *(adj.)*—Showy; intended to attract notice; **PRETENTIOUS** (DH Core)

199. **GUILE** *(n.)*—Treacherous cunning; skillful deceit; **DUPLICITY** (Word 110)

200. **SANGUINE** *(adj.)*—Cheerfully confident; optimistic

201. **SCINTILLATING** *(adj.)*—Sparkling; shining; brilliantly clever

202. **PRISTINE** *(adj.)*—Remaining in a pure state; uncorrupted by civilization

203. **RAMPANT** *(adj.)*—Unrestrained; unchecked

204. **PERNICIOUS** *(adj.)*—Highly **INJURIOUS** (Word 113); destructive; deadly

205. **OBLIVIOUS** *(adj.)*—Lacking conscious awareness; unmindful; unaware

206. **REFRACTORY** *(adj.)*—**RECALCITRANT** (DH Core); obstinately resistant to authority; hard to manage

207. **GARRULOUS, VERBOSE, LOQUACIOUS, VOLUBLE** *(adj.)*—Annoyingly talkative; speaking incessantly; babbling

208. **CONVIVIAL** *(adj.)*—Sociable; fond of feasting, drinking, and good company

209. **BRUSQUE, CURT** *(adj.)*—Abrupt in manner or speech; discourteously blunt

210. **TEPID** *(adj.)*—Lukewarm; mild; half-hearted

211. **PROTEAN** *(adj.)*—Readily taking on varied forms and meanings

212. **SOLICITOUS** *(adj.)*—Showing great care and concern; attentive

213. **INGENUOUS** *(adj.)*—Free from deviousness, innocent; **NAÏVE** (DH Essential); **GUILELESS**; **SINCERE** (DH Core)
DISINGENUOUS *(adj.)*—insincere; NOT candid; NOT straightforward; calculating; oblique

214. **VENERATE** *(adj.)*—To regard with great respect; to hold in high esteem

215. **CONTENTIOUS** *(adj.)*—Quarrelsome; argumentative; likely to provoke a controversy

216. **PRECLUDE** *(n.)*—To make impossible; to rule out; to prevent

217. **COMPUNCTION, CONTRITION, REMORSE, PENITENCE** *(n.)*—Feelings of **SINCERE** (DH Core) and deep regret

218. **DEMOGRAPHY** *(n.)*—The study of the characteristics of human populations

219. **APHORISM, AXIOM, MAXIM** *(n.)*—A statement universally accepted as true

220. **JUXTAPOSE** *(v.)*—To place side by side or in close proximity
JUXTAPOSITION *(n.)*—The position of being close together or side by side

221. **BOMBASTIC** *(adj.)*—**POMPOUS** (DH Core) or pretentious in speech or writing; **OSTENTATIOUSLY** (Word 198) lofty in style

222. **FORBEARANCE** *(n.)*—Abstaining from the enforcement of a right; the act of refraining from acting on a desire or impulse

223. **UNFETTERED** *(n.)*—Free of restraint of any kind; liberated

224. **PRESCRIBE** *(v.)*—To require; to order; to direct
PROSCRIBE *(v.)*—To forbid; to prohibit; to outlaw

225. **PUERILE, CALLOW, SOPHOMORIC** *(adj.)*—Childishly foolish; inexperienced; immature

226. **POLYMATH** *(n.)*—A person whose expertise spans a significant number of subject areas
DILETTANTE *(n.)*—An amateur or dabbler; a person with a **SUPERFICIAL** (DH Core) interest in an art or a branch of knowledge; a trifler

227. **DISSEMBLER, PREVARICATOR** *(n.)*—A liar and deceiver

Answer Keys

 CHAPTER 1

Great vigor or energy:

Word 1: panache

Word 2: verve

Word 3: flamboyance

Answers will vary for synonyms and sentences. Refer back to the definition to check your work.

 CHAPTER 2

Excessive desire for wealth:

Word 1: avarice

Word 2: cupidity

Word 3: covetousness

Very poor:

Word 1: destitute

Word 2: impoverished

Word 3: indigent

Answers will vary for definitions, synonyms, and sentences. Refer back to the definition to check your work.

 CHAPTER 3

Gravity:

Primary: natural force of attraction exerted by a celestial body

Secondary: seriousness; dignity; solemnity; weight

Bent:

Primary: twisted

Secondary: a strong tendency; a leaning; an inclination; a propensity

Eclipse:

Primary: total or partial covering of one celestial body by another

Secondary: to overshadow; to outshine; to surpass

Answers will vary for definitions, synonyms, and sentences. Refer back to the definition to check your work.

 # CHAPTER 4

Flexible:	**Future event; omen:**
Word 1: plastic	Word 1: harbinger
Word 2: malleable	Word 2: portent
Word 3: pliable	Word 3: presage

Answers will vary for definitions, synonyms, and sentences. Refer back to the definition to check your work.

CHAPTER 5

Ill-tempered:	**Insightful:**
Word 1: churlish	Word 1: perspicacious
Word 2: sullen	Word 2: prescient
Word 3: surly	Word 3: discerning

Answers will vary for definitions, synonyms, and sentences. Refer back to the definition to check your work.

INDEX